The Power of Shut Up

Published By: Pen Legacy®
Editing By: Shawn Mason
Formatting & Layout By: Junnita Jackson

DISCLAIMER

Although you may find the teachings, life lessons and examples in this book to be useful, the book is sold with the understanding that neither the author nor Pen Legacy® are engaged in presenting any legal, relationship, financial, emotional, or health advice.

Any person who's experiencing financial, anxiety, depression, health, or relationship issues should consult with a licensed therapist, advisor, licensed psychologist, or any qualified professional before commencing into anything described in this book. This book's intent is to provide you with the writer's account and experience with overcoming life matters. All results will differ than yours; however, our goal is to provide you with our "take" on how to overcome and be resilient when faced with circumstances. There are lessons in every blessing.

Library of Congress Cataloging – in- Publication Data has been applied for.

ISBN: 978-0-9600483-2-8

PRINTED IN THE UNITED STATES OF AMERICA.

Bible Verses about Shutting Up!

Proverbs 17:27-28

[27] Whoever restrains his words has knowledge, and he who has a cool spirit is a man of understanding. [28] Even a fool who keeps silent is considered wise; when he closes his lips, he is deemed intelligent.

Praise For Lisa Washington And The Power Of Shut Up

Lisa and I met at a Women's Fellowship that I host in MD. After the Service ended she shared some things she was going through. After she and I prayed, The Spirit of The Lord put it on my heart to share these words with her. "Be quiet and be still." There are times when some things should be confronted, then there are times when God simply wants us to be still and know He is God. (Scripture reference Psalm 46:10) Silence is not only a weapon but it is a sign of spiritual growth. Our ability to be quiet may confirm that we are interested in what is being said. It can also show that we have great integrity and will not be brought into conversations that could be harmful. Culture often influences our desire to have the last say. But as believers wisdom says sometimes saying nothing is more powerful than saying anything at all.

~ Stacy Lattisaw Jackson

I first met Lisa at a conference that I was hosting. I shared my story about how my big mouth almost ended my marriage and she shared with me that she could relate. Once I began coaching Lisa, I could see this process wasn't easy for her. She pushed back hard with tears in her eyes, yet I saw how she was willing to do the work. The will to shut up is HUGE! This book is a first-hand account of how learning to just be quiet and use wisdom with your words will strengthen you, make your relationships better and give you peace. Lisa put in the work and knows what she's talking about. I think any woman who wants to be in control of her emotions, her life should read this book and be open to learning The Power Of Shut

Up. I believe this book is going to save marriages all around the world. A much-needed message. Great job Lisa!

~ Gail Crowder

Contents

About the Book

Learning to shut up, for some people, is a very difficult task. That's because being quiet means taking away one's power to express their thoughts, emotions, and concerns. In this compelling story, filled with real-life situations and heartrendingly powerful truths of how "talking" too much can have an adverse effect on your life, love, and relationships, Lisa demonstrates why the Power of Shut Up is necessary.

Mastering this concept requires both a process and a practice that will be taught throughout this book through coaching, practical tips, and guided conversations. The Power of Shut Up will help you dig into your inner thoughts and discover why being heard is such a great accomplishment, but why listening can save you from unnecessary chaos. As you go through life, interacting with others, sharing your opinions, and making decisions, this book will help you think before you speak, but most importantly, think before you react.

I am going to share many examples and scenarios where shutting up was good and maybe not so good but through it all, the main lesson will be to understand that Shut Up has POWER!

Foreword

On every playground.

In every household.

Definitely at the office.

The words, "Shut Up!" are fighting words. Like throw on the ground, drag through the mud kinda fighting and yet, something about this phrase is powerful. Depending on who uses it, how and when.

When Lisa first told me about how she was going to write about the biggest, hardest challenge of her life, I was excited. Lisa and I met when I interviewed her on my radio show. Although we had never met in person (only talked on the phone once), it was something about her that was comforting, smart and open. The interview went well and I told her that her gift to gab reminds of someone else I know - who loves to talk, is outgoing and wants to see people win. Me.

Like me, Lisa loves to talk, to share and telling her to shut up? That was like cutting off her airwaves and expecting her to breathe Yet, the advice, those usual fighting words, helped to shape Lisa into the powerful media expert that she is today.

By reading The Power of Shut Up, you are going to learn a vital skill that most people think is offensive, restricting and yet, it is needed in today's culture of Twitter beefs, cyberbullying and internet trolls. I appreciate that Lisa

2

isn't just telling us what to do, but she's showing us how it is done step-by step.

Because of our similarities, Lisa and I became friends quickly. She was the producer for my weekly radio show and she helped to produce our first television broadcast, It's All About Love. During her time as a producer, she was a newlywed, a mom and a step-mom, as well as, a magazine publisher. When she asked me to write the Foreword for the book, I was honored.

The Power of Shut Up is a necessary tool for both men and women, various ages who grew up to believe that "If I got something to say, I just gotta say it." Words are powerful and not everything needs to be said especially if your intent or attitude isn't right. The valuable lessons that Lisa weaves into her own process of learning The Power of Shut Up are timeless.

The sections of The Power of Shut Up are broken down so that you can locate yourself on your journey of being a better communicator. Lisa shares how she grew up being taught, like many women, girls are to be seen and not heard. If you weren't raised like that, you will understand the struggle of being confronted with a difficult situation, like racism in the school hallway, and how to deal with the situation properly and...not so properly. Lisa's transparency in The Power of Shut Up gives us hope that no matter where we are - on the job, in relationships, in public settings - that we can learn to hold our peace by closing our mouths.

I recommend The Power Of Shut Up to anyone who has a little diarrhea of the mouth or for any of you who wants so badly to say to someone...please Shut Up! A joy to read and many lessons to be learned. I hope millions of people, young and old, will learn The Power of Shut Up.

~ Shawn Mason

Introduction

As a child, I was quiet most of the time. I rarely said much when I was around people outside of my immediate family. Some of that was because I was an observer. But I also felt that my voice didn't matter. Then I progressed to a place where I had no filter. I was rebelling from being silent and passive almost daily. I had something to say about any and everything and you couldn't get me to shut up at all. I felt like I was speaking up to make up for all those years that I never said much. I had to stand up for myself but I would even take it a step further, I stood up for everyone else too. If you did something that I felt was wrong to somebody else, I had something to say about that too. I had grown tired of feeling like I was being overlooked and taken advantage of because I didn't say anything. I would see people speaking up and saying whatever they felt they needed to say and now it was my turn. But there was a method to this madness that I was unaware of at the time, but I would soon find out because life was happening and lessons were waiting. I was going to learn today!

I had to learn that to be heard doesn't mean you have to be loud, nor does it mean that you have to be unkind. Communication is not always spoken and it can be meaningless without learning how to do it. I learned that everything you say doesn't have to come out of your mouth, (boy, was that a hard one). There is a definite balance that has to be used when communicating with anyone and once you start to figure that out, conversations and interactions with others become much more productive and meaningful.

I would watch people speak their mind and say how they felt, heck...even cuss folks out sometimes, and they always seemed to not have a care in the world, nor did that care what others thought or said about them when they did, and in some way, I admired that. But why did I admire that? Why couldn't I speak up and defend myself? Why did I care what others would think if I did? The way I was talking to myself played a major part too. I would block myself by saying things like, "Who am I to be speaking up?", "What could I say about anything that others didn't already know?" "Who do I think I am?". All those words played in my mind constantly and played a major role in how I learned to communicate with people. Throughout my journey I had to learn that the way I talked to myself as well as the way I talked to others was extremely important. How did I want to communicate with others? Did I want to say what I wanted without a care in the world or did I want to hold back and let the way others felt guide the way I chose to communicate. Decisions, Decisions.

I would learn that words can sometimes make or break a friendship, relationship, etc. and more importantly, I would learn during this journey that words are permanent, and you can't take them back. There is power in the tongue and if you don't learn how to control it, you can truly hurt others as well as yourself in many instances, and I will share with you how I learned that the hard way.

Because I had not figured things out yet about how and when to speak up, there were many times when I felt less than, weak, dismissed, because I knew all too well how to shut up & be quiet, but the question was, was that always the best answer? Did I want to be heard or understood? Was there a difference?

Growing up you would often hear that children were supposed to be seen, not heard. My mom had never put those specific restraints on my sister and I but we did understand that every conversation wasn't for children. And to be honest, sometimes we forgot our place and, our mother put us back in our place. You know what I mean. You know what your mother or grandmother meant when she would say things like, "You are smelling yourself", right? That meant that you were being sassy, smart at the mouth, being grown, and you were probably about to get my butt whooped. I know many of you can relate. That was my situation many times when I "forgot my place" and thought I could speak my mind because I was in my, "I ain't being quiet no more" period of my life. Well, let's just say, momma don't play that so she quickly reminded me, lol. I was so busy running my mouth and embracing my power of speech that I forgot that I wasn't grown yet and my mother wasn't having it.

And then we have those times when the power can be used as a weapon. We all know that friend or spouse, or family member, maybe even one of your children will try it, (and I say "try" loosely of course) lol, or it might even be us that uses their silence to punish or prove a point. Yes, we have all done it and some of us are very good at it as a matter of fact. It is a weapon of choice for a lot of people. But did you ever think about what you got out of it? Sure, immediately you got some relief from the conversation or you pissed the other person off and made them feel bad. Was that what you wanted to accomplish? What was your goal? Did things get better with that situation or did they just come to a stand still only to arise again once you spoke again? hmmm. But let's call it what it is, (Watch those toes ;-)) It's PETTY!

Yes petty, I said it! 😳 Keep in mind, when I am sharing my journey of learning how and when to be quiet and Shut Up, I am also sharing with you how the power can be misused and abused. Any power that you have can be taken advantage of and misused to hurt, upset or taunt others and that is one of those moments when a self #chincheck is in order. We all have to be careful with the power we have and we should always make sure that our intentions are good when using them. The Power of Shut Up is a strong power that can be used for good and bad and we must know the difference between the two.

It was a little scary writing this book at times, partly because it was embarrassing to share how weak I felt. There was also a shame attached to realizing that I still had those moments as an adult. Even though some things happened so many years ago during my childhood, it was still happening to me as a grown woman on a larger scale. I was finding myself in situations where I was retreating back to those quiet moments where I would choose to say nothing because I didn't want to disrespect a relative or in-law or I didn't want to rock the boat in my relationship, but it was building up inside an actually making me sick at times. I was harboring hurt, resentment, sickness and sadness at times because I wouldn't say what was on my mind or what I was thinking. I didn't want to be "the complainer", "the mean one", "the difficult one", or (this one was a big one for me) "the confrontational one", but something had to give. There had to be a balance to this. I had to learn that method that they speak of to this madness I was experiencing and quick because I was making myself sick, frustrated and unhappy a lot of the times in my relationships and feeling totally misunderstood practically all of the time. I had to make some changes.

There were so many turning points in my life where I was responding and reacting totally unaware of the consequences of my actions. I felt the need to write this book because over the years I have learned so much about the importance of communication and that although we have the right to speak, there is a time and a place for everything. It is not just the fact that because you can speak, upi just do, it's more about the responsibility you have to figure out how, when, where and even if you should speak. I figured out that I was communicating of course, but I wasn't communicating well. I wasn't being heard, and I a lot of times I was being totally misunderstood. I had to learn the balance between being quiet and speaking up and I also had to understand why that was necessary.

We have all been in situations, whether it be friendships, relationships, work interactions, public interactions, kids, family, blended family relationships and the list goes on and on, where we have to learn how to communicate effectively. Throughout your entire life you will have to address people regarding good and bad situations and you will have to find a way to have that conversation in a mature and productive way or maybe not have that conversation at all but this book will hopefully serve as a guide to help you through those predicaments and give you tips on how to approach difficult situations. I hope that this book will even give you a different perspective about the words shut up and grow to a place where you are not as insulted about shutting up and sometimes you will even agree that is the best thing to do!

We all probably have the same reaction when we hear the words "SHUT UP". When I would hear the words Shut Up, I was "whippin' my head around like Willow Smith whipped her hair" because I just knew somebody must have gotten confused about who you were talking to. Y'all know what I'm talking about.

Let's be clear, being quiet or shutting up does not mean that you don't have a voice. The Power of Shut Up comes as a journey or process where you learn if, when and how you should express yourself through words. This power will help you to strengthen your discernment and increase your focus. Now don't get me wrong, this journey is in no way easy and it is an indefinite learning process, meaning, you will never stop being a student in this process, and neither will I. You will reach highs and lows along the way and sometimes forget what you know to be the right way because emotions, circumstances and life will alter all that in a hot minute, but the great thing about learning how to hone in on your power of shut up is that you get better at catching yourself, and you catch yourself a whole lot earlier and eventually easier, lol. I learned how to re-direct, hold on a little tighter or release my Shut Up power appropriately along this journey.

In this book, I hope to teach others how to think before you speak and check your intentions. You sometimes need to even check your source because people will impose on you and you have to start to know when that is happening. I hope to enlighten you about if, when and how but I also am excited about sharing my insights on why. Knowing why the Power of Shut up is important will help to keep you aware when things get challenging.

Thank you for joining me on this journey and I hope that you use this publication as a guide through life to help you through those moments when you don't know what to say, how to say it, when to say or even if you should say it!

Quiet Little Girl

I grew up quiet with not much to say but a lot on my mind. I was never a big talker as a child, even to the point that some of my family thought I was kind of mean at times, because I never had anything to say. Boy did they have me all wrong.

First of all, let me say, I was not mean, at least I don't think I was. Well, it depends on who you ask. Secondly, I had plenty to say but had little to no nerve to say it. I was always way too concerned about what people would think. The concern for people's feelings kept me from speaking up most of the time.

As a young girl, I was actually a Tomboy at heart. I loved playing with frogs and turtles and would climb a tree in a minute. I never thought of myself as a pretty girl. I was ok with being more like an "ugly duckling"! I loved playing sports and never wanted to wear a dress, I mean NEVER! I remember times when I would be bullied or teased and the target was usually my great big eyes. I was teased constantly and called names like, "Bubble Eyes", "Big Eyes" and "Cat Eyes", just to name a few. I rarely spoke up to defend myself.

My feelings were hurt and I cried. I just wasn't sure of all of the emotions. Was I more hurt that someone was calling me names or was I angrier that I was too scared to stand up for myself? Either way, I stayed silent.

Inside of my head, I was yelling and shouting at the top of my lungs. I never liked being around a lot of chaos and confusion. To me if I said something, chaos and confusion were sure to follow. I made it a habit to not bring drama to any situation, so I avoided stuff that would lead to drama. I would gradually start to see that my decision, or choice to stay silent would show up and had become how I dealt with stuff. The times that encountered teasing and bullying as a child, I stayed quiet. I was always misunderstood and judged. My facial expressions were usually interpreted wrong. I was just shy and trying to figure everything out in my head. Because my usual was 'stay quiet,' I couldn't express myself to anyone when I was touched by a neighbor inappropriately at the young age of 11. I didn't even tell my mother, the person closest to me for almost 40 years.

As far back as I can remember, my mom had always taught my sister and I that she had our back. She told us that we could come and talk to her about anything in the world, but the reality is, when things happen to you, you may not believe what you're told. You can be taught all the right, appropriate things to do in any given situation and sometimes you will still choose to do the very opposite. The reasons vary but for me, I didn't want to disrupt my world or cause any confusion. I didn't want to bring any chaos into my life or anyone else's, so I stayed quiet.

When I would be teased as a child about how big my eyes were or the fact that I wasn't cute, or a was a tomboy, it

13

always hurt. Silence seemed to be the best response. When there was a party that was happening, but I didn't make the guest list, I stayed quiet. When you tried to do the right thing and just treat others as you wanted to be treated, but, they still mistreated you, yes, it hurt. I had learned to keep my feelings hidden deep inside which only increased that pain I felt. My silence was affecting my self-esteem in a major way. The decisions about when or when not to speak had affected my whole life.

I will share a situation or two that will sound very familiar to some and brand new to others that involve issues related to bullying and racism among other things. The reason I chose to share some of these experiences as examples is because these shaped and molded me in how I showed up in the world as a youth. It also helps to show examples of how young people sometimes lose their voice long before they even start to learn how to use it. Those very moments when you sometimes blew off an incident between kids as child's play or minimized an argument between friends, could very well be the pinpoint time when that child lost their voice or lost faith in someone words. When kids are bullied and made to feel less than, they retreat and internalize what's happening and many times they become distant and silent. There were many times when I felt like, one voice, MY voice, would never make a difference so what was the point. There were many times where I felt like silence was the best response for all the wrong reasons and I even remained silent for a very long time. The choice to stay silent sometimes would many times seem like the right thing to do at the time but later in life, what I didn't realize is that it would show up in ways that I could have never predicted. Being silent and shutting up had real repercussions for me as a young girl, and it would prove almost 40 years later to still have an effect on my life as an adult.

Shutting up became my way to deal with things and internalizing them became my way to cope with many things and that would prove to be a bad recipe. The bad part was that I learned to carry it and carry it well, (so I thought). I didn't have an understanding of the weight or depth that went along with my silence, not just for me but for others who would cross my path or who may have encountered the same situation I had encountered. I developed a habit of remaining silent in times of pain to avoid being criticized, judged or even accused of lying and I didn't want to cause problems for others, "A people pleaser" in the making, but unseen to most.

I didn't want to fight, I didn't want to upset anyone, and I didn't want to make people unhappy, but I must admit, I was paying the price without even knowing it because I was the unhappy one. I retreated many times because I had not learned to fight for my voice, not because I wasn't taught to, but because at home I never had to. I had not exercised that ability, so I was unaware of how to use it.

Of course, there were many times that I wanted to speak but didn't, and that truly made me angry. We have all had those moments when we were challenged with the decision to speak up about something that you just knew wasn't right, but there were so many things that went along with that choice, and if you weren't ready to deal with the aftermath, you chose to say nothing. And let's keep in mind, there were rules that applied to you as a child that prohibited you from saying just anything you might have wanted to say to anybody, and if you did, Oh boy, you were going to be in serious trouble! You would sometimes hear things like, "Shut Your Mouth", "That's not your place" or "I will handle this, you be quiet". It just never seemed to be an appropriate time to "Speak Up" but it always seemed to be a right time to "Shut Up" at least that is what I thought as a child.

I had developed an opinion about being quiet. I didn't like it even though I always did it. I thought that being quiet was not really a good thing at all. In my opinion, people would walk all over you, make assumptions about you that were wrong, be negative towards you for no reason, and mistreat you, when you kept your mouth shut. It made me feel unimportant, different, (and not in a good way), and it even made me feel very lonely at times. I was pushed, teased and tested and I believed that people treated me that way because they viewed me as weak, timid and incapable of defending myself. Silence was not my friend!

On top of that, I had issues with perception, and I didn't want to appear difficult or a "pain in the butt", so I rarely commenting on things or added my opinion and kept quiet. I went along with the crowd and the program most of the time, it just seemed easier that way. I guess you could say that I was a follower in a sense. Although I never thought of myself as a follower back then, hindsight is 20/20 so maybe I was. I thought pretending to be a follower was much less confusion than not so shutting up became my thing!

I was the type of person that wanted to see everyone happy. I would usually say yes to just about anything you asked to me to do, even if I didn't want to. I mean, I wouldn't do anything that would get me hurt, but if someone asked me could they use my bike even though that would leave me sitting on the curb, or asked me to give them some money at the ice cream truck that left me with less than what I needed to get what I wanted, 9 times out of 10, I still did it, with very little hesitation. It just seemed easier and like I said before, I didn't want any drama. I didn't want people thinking I was selfish and stingy. It was no big deal, right? My mom always taught me to share and be kind. So why not? But was that true? How did I feel inside?

I wanted to say NO many times, but I could never seem to drudge up the courage to do it, and again, I didn't want to be mean or make people think that I wasn't a team player. No seemed to be such a cold word to me and I could never find a reason why I could just go ahead and do whatever it was. I had not yet learned that no is not a dirty word. All these things were teaching me that communication is important at any given age and at a young age is where you learn how to communicate. All the experiences that you go through in life teach you how to relate to others and receive what they say to you as well. Some learn how to communicate by watching others, some learn by listening, while others learn by both. And I will have to admit, we all learn about how to interact in a very different ways, and looking back on it, we sometimes received very confusing messages regarding how to use your words and how to communicate your feelings to others. See, the rules change the older you get, and I realized that there were times when you were told to do one thing and maybe shown something different or vice versa. Sometimes as kids, we didn't know how to respond because the message was mixed and the main thing, we wanted to make sure didn't happen was, we didn't want is to get in any kind of trouble?

Here are some examples of mixed messages we receive through our younger days that may have caused some confusion. Do some of these mixed messages sound confusing to you? Check these out…….

Remember when your parents or an adult would say things like,
"Speak only when spoken to." But at the same time you were told, "You betta speak when you walk into a room."

How about this one?
"Don't be stingy and share." But you would also hear, "It's ok to say no sometimes"

And then there was this one.
"Don't ever disrespect an adult." But at the same time you were told, "If someone does something, you need to speak up."

And finally is this one which I happen to think is one of the biggest mixed messages that so many parents are guilty of….
"You don't have to yell and scream to get your point across." But in the same breathe, parents will yell and scream at the kids when telling kids to do something.

I know, I know, it can get very confusing, I agree. Life is about communication and it starts even before you leave the womb. This book is to share the importance of understanding our words and why we communicate the way we do. What we learn while we are young truly does guide the way we interact with others as we grow older. My goal is to help you to recognize those triggers and situations that you experienced or even your children will experience in life that will influence you in positive and negative ways. Being aware is the first step to be able to do something to change the behavior. There will be times in your life when communication gets cloudy and how to react or respond in any given situation could truly make a difference in your life. My hope is that as I reflect and share the things that I have gone through even as a child, I can better help you understand why you chose to speak or not speak up about things and how those decisions that probably seemed so small then, could have actually changed the course of your life in many ways. Somethings you won't be able to go back and change but, in many cases, as in mine, understanding why, made a serious impact on how I proceeded going forward.

But, keeping my mouth shut seemed to be getting me nowhere most of the time and I never felt good when I did. Instead, I felt invisible. I felt like no one could hear me or cared to hear me either. No one cared what my opinion was, let alone wanted to hear anything I had to say but I was growing sick and tired of being silent, not being heard and dismissed and decided that it was time for a change, at least that is what I told myself.

REFLECTIONS

How did your childhood or how you were raised impact your voice, your willingness to speak up? Was your confidence/self-esteem impacted? In the beginning I spoke about being quiet, never saying much, worried about hurting someone's feeling by what I said or getting in trouble with my parents.

Write examples of how you stayed quiet about some things that happened around you or to you in your life. How did it make you feel? Do you wish you had said something or were you scared to speak? Did holding your peace make you upset, angry, sad?

_____

_____

_____

_____

_____

_____

_____

_____

_____

_____

_____

_____

_____

_____

_____

_____

_____

_____

From DC to the Real South

Sometimes you have no choice and sometimes it's just a matter of choice. My mother and father were getting a divorce and my mother had decided to take a job in Georgia. But I had friends that I had grown up with since 2nd and 3rd grade so this change was going to be major for me. I had friends that I played with in school and at home all my life while I was growing up and my life was good. I didn't want that to change, but as a young person, many times, you have absolutely no choice in the matter. Not only that but something new and different like living in another state and going to a whole new school was scary, maybe even terrifying and I was nervous and anxious. I was shy and quiet remember? So, as far as I could see, this transition was not going to be a good one at all, but again, I had no voice, I mean, I had no choice. My mom was moving, so I was too.

Now to add insult to injury, when we 1st moved to Georgia I was headed to the 7th grade because back home in Maryland I had just graduated from the 6th grade and out of elementary school. Well, now that I was in Georgia, that was not the case. Georgia schools in the area we moved to had elementary school up until 7th grade which meant that I was actually headed back to elementary school AGAIN! (ugh) I was supposed to be going to Junior High School like all of my friends back home. But what could I say? Nothing. This was how it was going to be and as a kid, what can you say. But I was a trooper. I wanted to share with my mom that I didn't want to go, I had wished that she had included me in the decision making, of course. But we all know that there will be times in your life when you have to deal with the hand you're dealt. And on top of that, I was just a kid and I knew that my mom was doing what was best for us, and I wasn't about to make her feel bad or get angry, and I certainly didn't want to make things difficult or rock the boat. So again, I went along with the program. I held my feeling and fears inside and kept it moving. New environment and surroundings that were very different from where I grew up, yep, I would be challenged.

So, let me share with you a story that would challenge me and the way my voice showed up in the world. I mentioned that my mom moved to Georgia back when I was headed to the 7th grade right? See, when I was growing up in Maryland, believe it or not, I grew up in mixed community and I had friends of all nationalities during my elementary school days. Some may call it sheltered, but I had never run into any issues related to the color of my skin or anything like that, until I moved down south. There was no racism in my immediate world back at home that I was aware of and in my world, everyone liked everyone, and everyone got along great for the most part. Life seemed wonderful, and of course

23

it did, because I didn't know any better lol. But Georgia was about to teach me something new and awaken my voice in a way that I was not expecting. I was in for a rude awakening. Life as I knew it was about to change, and I was about to learn some real-life lessons, almost instantly.

There are so many stories that I can share with you where I was challenged consistently in regards to responding to things that were shown to be totally disrespectful and even unprovoked while living in the south and the fact that I had never encountered things like this before, made my adjustments that much harder. I can't share them all but a couple of things I will share will surely help you get the jist of some of my challenges along the way.

I had finally completed 7th grade and went on the 8th grade, (middle school). That shy and quiet girl that existed for so long was about to change. I was started to grow tired of always going along with the program and my silence was about to be broken. I changed my whole attitude about being quiet. Some might call it a rebellious stage but I prefer to call it a stage of awareness. At least that is how I justified my behavior at the time. I was aware that I had something to say that mattered and I was no longer scared to share. I was tired of being taken advantage of and being quiet, taking mess off folks and being pushed around. I didn't feel like shutting up anymore. The weight was getting heavier and I was pushing back. Pushing back HARD! Being quiet didn't feel good to me, it made me feel smothered, weak, insignificant, and I didn't want that feeling any more. I no longer wanted to be pushed around and decided that EVERYTHING was worth speaking up and fighting for, Oh MY!

In my eyes, it seemed like those who spoke up were talked about badly, yes, but they seemed to be so free after they spoke up. They never seemed to care what others thought about them and I wanted that feeling. I wanted to not care either. They weren't worried about anyone else's feelings and they seemed happier. Why wouldn't I want a piece of that action? I was tired of being overlooked and not counted. I wanted to be seen and in my eyes, in order to be seen, I had to be heard and heard loud and clear. I spoke up about anything and everything because I was determined to let it be known that I was not going to be pushed around anymore. In my eyes, I had ARRIVED, I was not going to be mistreated anymore and people were going to know how I felt, period, so I thought. I spoke up for me, I spoke up for friends, I spoke up for everyone, sounds like a good thing right. Maybe, maybe not.

I guess I thought I was as they say, "Keeping it REAL"....lol.

I spoke up about everything, and I mean everything.

I recall a time while I was in middle school and again, I had to get used to being in a new school and making all new friends. I was still adjusting to living down south and trying to get used to the culture and challenges of being black in a place where racism was very much still alive and well. I had only been living there for a short while, but I was experiencing some real culture shocks. While attending this new middle school, I quickly figured out that I was one of ONLY four black students in the entire school which was already intimidating, and on top of that I was the fairest/lightest African American student of the three which I would soon find out and would prove to be an additional challenge.

I walked the halls of the school daily, uncomfortable, but remember, I was rebelling...I wasn't taking no stuff off nobody. I remember it like it was yesterday, I had been in my favorite class with my favorite teacher, English class of course, imagine that, and had to go to the restroom. As most schools did, you had to get permission to leave the classroom to go, so I did. You remember, you had to have a hall pass or you were in trouble, well, I did as I was supposed to and headed out the classroom. Just minutes after entering the hallway, I was approached by another student who happened to be Caucasian, but apparently felt some kind of way about black people and felt he had to share his feelings about the fact that I was black. He passed by me, slowing down and he passed by and said, "Get out of my way you Nigger", which truly caught me off guard so in response I said, "Excuse me", I was totally confused by why this was happening right now.

I had never had any problems with anyone at the school and I had never messed with anyone, although I always felt a little uncomfortable being the minority, But I was totally lost at that moment. In turn he responded to me saying, "You heard me Jungle Bunny"! Wow, was this happening? Did he just call me a jungle bunny? (*Side Note: Georgia is a warm state and people get some fabulous tans down there and the young man that was speaking to me was actually darker than me because he had a GREAT tan, go figure*).

Did I mention that while he was calling me a jungle bunny, he was also swinging his jacket at me, to hit me with it? Now, remember, I had started to already release my new-found power of speaking up because shutting up wasn't

26

serving me well, so this could have gone so many ways. If I felt someone was being wronged, I spoke up, even if it wasn't my battle. I took on everything that I thought was wrong or every wrong-doing I witnessed to others, not paying attention to the fact that I was building a reputation for being all the things that I feared as a child, difficult, miserable, lonely and mean.

Back to the hallway action, nobody was going to talk to me like that and certainly not swing things at me. I grabbed the jacket and proceeded to snatch it out of his hands while responding right back with, "Who are you think you talking' to? Your momma is a......., (you get the message). I was a teenager so the words I was spouting off were foul to say the least, but I had no power over my words at that moment. I had totally lost it. Yelling at the top of my lungs, hurt and angry, I believe I actually caught him off guard because his face looked like he was in total shock and he froze in that moment. There was so much happening all at once and it wasn't over because simultaneously I was looking to strike back, not only with my tongue but with my hands on too! But before I could smack the crap out of him, my teacher came running into the hallway, "What in the world is going on here?"

I honestly to this day, still believe that she actually heard the confusion in the hallway (all those nasty words that I was called) before she ran into the hallway and saw it because when she looked into my eyes, without saying one word to me, she sent him straight to the Principal's office, and I had not explained anything that had taken place yet. The student in question didn't even object because I think he assumed she heard us too, and he knew he was wrong. As he walked away, I stood there, not sure what was about to happen, because I too said some inappropriate things, but I am not even sure I cared because I was so heated that I couldn't even speak. Tears rolling down my face, partly because I was hurt, but mostly because I was mad as hell, I just dropped the jacket and looked at her, ready for what was to come. She walked me to the restroom and told me to take whatever time I needed. I did just that and then went back to class. Of course, this threw off my whole day, but I shared it with no one until I got home. Then it was time to tell momma. Oh my!!!! I shared with my mom what happened and yes, I gave her all the details, what he did and what I did.

My mother was a no-nonsense kind of woman and I always admired the way she spoke up when she felt she needed to, and that is what I thought I was doing too. I wanted to use my voice just like her, but in that moment I didn't. I felt bad, not because I had defended myself, but more because I was taken out of my character and I had allowed someone to totally steal my joy. This event had disrupted my entire day and I was unproductive for the remainder of the day. My mother did take me back to school that very next morning and made sure that the school knew how she felt about what had happened. She also made it clear that the student needed to be handled and that should never happen again and she communicated all of that to them with a great sense of authority in a classy way. She taught them a lesson or two, but, the biggest lesson was getting ready to be taught to me. I know some of you might think, Lisa, you did exactly what I would have done. Some of you might have even done more, I get it, but it wasn't about that for my mom.

Her concern of course was first about how I was feeling about what happened and she wanted to make sure that I knew that what someone says about you doesn't make it true. But she also wanted me to understand that I should never allow him or anyone else to take me out of my space and steal my peace or joy. When you respond to ignorance in like, you lower yourself to their standard. I started to understand the power of words and how I wanted to use my voice. That situation showed me how easy it is to get caught up in bad behavior and let it take you from who you are. Yes, I vented and said what I felt, that part is true. But, it also drained me of my energy and focus and stole time out of my day that I could have used for other positive things that were going on. This was the beginning of a real turning point in my life as a young adult where I was starting to recognize how your voice and what you say and how you say it absolutely frames how you show up in the world. I started to understand that there is a balance that has to be learned and that you will be tested and sometimes you will respond out of emotion, and that doesn't mean you are necessarily wrong, but it does mean that when you do, you may say things that you can't take back. This would not be my last test by any means but it had shown me what can happen when you respond to foolishness and how it can make you feel inside. I thought it would have felt good, and as a matter of fact, it did for a quick minute, but when I came down from that instant gratification, I felt like i had been hit by a ton of bricks because I wasn't responding in my best voice.

REFLECTIONS

Could you have done something differently that would have changed the outcome of the situation? If you didn't say anything, what would have happened?

_____

_____

_____

_____

_____

_____

_____

_____

_____

_____

_____

_____

_____

_____

_____

_____

_____

_____

_____

_____

_____

_____

_____

_____

And I Rise Up

Life was changing and I was getting older. Life was looking really different to me now. Being quiet and staying quiet was a thing of the past but I was aware that I couldn't just say anything out of my mouth. I was started to gain a lot of confidence and no longer afraid of what people would think if I shared what was on my mind, in a positive way of course. I was starting to manage my voice and become more aware of the power I had over my words and responses. But, there were still so many lessons to be learned and so many tests that were to come my way so although I was more aware, I still had a lot to learn. I hope that my transparency throughout the book will help you to understand that this is not an overnight lesson but I lifetime one.

As you get older, the lessons change, and you gain even more clarity on the power you possess with your voice. For starters, I recall a specific incident when I was on my designated neighborhood bus, headed home after school with all the kids who lived in my neighborhood or close to me. The bus was making its' rounds from neighborhood to neighborhood. Some of the kids were nice and spoke but again, there were other kids that weren't very nice and made it quite clear that they didn't even want to sit next to you. Because I was new to this kind of treatment because I had never experienced things like this before, it was a little difficult at times, but I had started to learn to ignore ignorance. I was claiming some control over my voice in that I choose not to address people who didn't want anything to do with me, partly because it made me angry and partly because I just didn't know how to react. Everyone was talking, laughing and just happy to be headed home, and as long as I was around and sitting with the friends that I knew, I was too. I was just as anxious as everyone else to go outside and play! (I know you didn't think I was going to say do homework, lol).

Like I was saying, on this day I was headed home on the bus after school enjoying the company of my friends from the neighborhood, excited to get home. Now to put things into perspective, there were only three black kids that rode our bus at this time. Make note that I was the only black student on the bus that day because the only other black student that rode the bus that day, didn't come to school. But that didn't faze me so much until this day and then everything changed. Now, the other young lady was a dark-skinned young lady and unlike me, she was very boisterous about everything. (this will become relevant shortly). She spoke her mind about everything whether it was right, wrong, kind or mean. She was not scared to say anything to anyone and had somewhat created a reputation of being bossy and intimidating. Most would not challenge her and wouldn't say anything bad about her, but I could tell that it wasn't out of respect, but more out of fear.

While talking and laughing with the other students on the bus, one of the young girl turns and says to me, "I really like you because you are light, you don't yell and fuss at everyone all the time". Wait what? What did she just say to me? I couldn't believe what she had just said to me. I was instantly angry. I felt totally disrespected in that moment and wanted to snatch her hair out of her head, better yet, punch her in the face, but I didn't, and I was angry with myself for not doing it. This was a WOW moment for me to say the least.

I reacted after a few minutes of sitting in total silence with no response to her. Then I found the words and asked, "You like me because I am light-skin? Is that what you just said? and without letting her respond I went on.," well, if that's the only reason you like me, then I don't like you." I had just realized that she was equating loud and mean to dark skin and quiet and nice to light-skin. I had mixed feelings about what had just happened. I was turned off by the loud talking and mean girl behavior as well, and I could see how that would turn someone off, but, to connect that to the color of her skin and decide that you would rather be friends with a light-skinned person because of what and how they said it was wrong, but it was REAL! Think about it. It was a real wake up call for me. I was slowly realizing that there was a definite balance that is necessary in speaking to someone. Although we were kids and it was an "out of the mouth of babes" situation, at the same time it was a huge realization about how people are perceived based on communication. I was getting a clear picture of how you will be judged and perceived based on how you communicate with people. I

34

wanted to yell, scream and possibly smack her to be honest. But what would that solve? How would that make the situation better? I had never seen my mother behave inappropriately when she was disrespected, so I kept it was short and firm.

See, my mother was a very outspoken, intelligent, no-nonsense woman and I admired that about her, but when she responded to ignorance, wrongdoing or disrespect, she always handled it with grace and class and it worked. Her control and strength in how she addressed people is what I admired. I would watch my mom in day to day activity as we encountered racism pretty much on a regular. The South was definitely a different culture for us, and I don't think I was ready, but I was about to learn.

We would go out on the weekends during that 1st summer that we moved down there and it was a must that we find out where the best places were to go shopping or bowling or roller skating, you know, whatever families do for enjoyment. I was starting to enjoy the new adventure that we were on and embrace the change. Maybe this situation was just one of those bad moments in time, so I gave it another try. Riding up the road checking out the sites along the way we ran across something that would totally disrupt my world.

Passing out leaflets on the median of the road was none other than members of the Ku Klux Klan, fully robed in white. Instantly I was scared. I was old enough to know what I was looking at but was totally confused about why I was seeing this with my own eyes. This was something I read about in our History books, my mom may have lived through this kind of thing but Not me. What a terrifying moment, that I would never ever forget. I wanted to speak out, shout out and let them know how stupid they were, how angry I was and how wrong what they were doing was but, I was scared, I was only a child and I wasn't sure what would happen to me, on top of that, as a child, wouldn't that be disrespectful? I mean, they were adults doing this, not kids. But my mom was cool calm and collected. Never flinched and never let it stop her or scare her. She continued to drive and never skipped a beat. I called my mother a "trooper" because to me, she was not scared of nothing or nobody and we were going to live wherever they wanted us there or not.

There was another time when my mom took my sister and I shopping at a nearby mall one weekend, one of our favorite pastimes, even today. We went to one of our favorite stores, I think it was maybe a retail clothing store that had a jewelry department inside. We strolled over to the jewelry counter to check out their necklaces and bracelets, my mom always wore beautiful jewelry and liked nice things, I was in awe of every piece in the display. My mother, my sister and I patiently waited a few steps back because the woman at the counter was helping another customer with some jewelry, but I would be lying if I didn't say I was anxious to be next because I was hoping I might get something, lol. You know how we do when momma is paying. So maybe about 10 minutes go by and the customer ahead of us leaves the counter, but before we could take a step closer, another customer came out of nowhere and walked right up to the counter.

The part that was disturbing was that the woman behind the counter, proceeded to assist her knowing that we had been standing there patiently for 10 minutes. Immediately I was pissed and proceeded to say, (very loud and sassy I might add) "EXCUSE ME, We were next, how are you going to assist that lady first, you know you saw us standing here", looking at my mother for an "AMEN" of course, but as graciously as I have ever seen it done, My mother gives me a look that lets me know, this ain't my battle and (SHE GOT THIS) and she proceeded to say, (in a calm voice) "Excuse me ma'am (directly to the customer) we were standing here waiting to be helped by this young lady but I am sure once she is finished helping us, she would be more than happy to help you". Then she turned to the woman behind the counter and said, "I would like to take a look at that necklace right there, thank you", pointing to the beautiful piece we were admiring prior to the confusion. That taught me a lot.

It taught me how to stay respectful but stand firm. I saw a situation where something was wrong and disrespectful, but my mom didn't shout, get loud or act a fool, she was classy and cool. I admired that in her. She was able to demand respect in such a graceful way. There were so many times while living down south that I was challenged with this very thing. It was definitely a culture shock for me and I was unclear many times on how to approach the situation and still get my point across. The hard part was that I was not used to this because growing up in Washington DC, (the chocolate city) and Maryland, I had never had to deal with this kind of thing. I grew up with people of all nationalities and I had never witnessed hate and disrespect at all. It had never crossed my path, and now I was thrown straight into the mix with no practice.

I experienced times when people made strong assumptions about what they could say to me because I was quiet. Sometimes it was good assumptions and sometimes bad, but nonetheless, they were assumptions and we all know what you make out of yourself when you assume right? lol. The more people challenged me because of my quietness, the more frustrated I became. I was growing up and didn't even realize it. Life was teaching me many things but one of the main things it was teaching me was how to find my voice and how to use it.

I was learning that being loud doesn't necessarily mean you are being heard and being silent doesn't always mean you are not heard. You can say much without moving your lips and you can say much of nothing moving them. The reality is that you will constantly be challenged by things that will cause you to react in a way that you may regret later but learning to how to think about the consequences of your actions and actually not letting other people's ignorance guide your responses is a great lesson. Two wrongs do not make a right, it's true, and sometimes realizing that makes the decision to respond in a more mature way, the hardest thing you will ever have to do. I was starting to understand the importance of my reaction in that moment. I had to decide what I would accomplish by reacting in a negative way to negative things and if it what I would gain in the end. I was finding my voice and starting to acknowledge and understand that there was power in words. I was becoming more aware of the influence that words have and I was making the connections in regards to how and when you should say things. I was starting to take a second to think about what I was about to say.

Words have consequences! No matter what, you must understand that whatever you say and how you say will always have repercussions, sometimes there will be good and positive things that come from it and sometimes not. But as you get older, you get to make that decisions and it starts to get harder to blame someone else for your actions and decisions. To be honest, I was slowly discovering that what came out of my mouth was all about me and less about others. With age comes wisdom and with wisdom come responsibility and along with all the other things that happen when you start to grow older, you also lose things too. You no longer get to blame all your responses and behaviors on someone else. I was learning that no matter what someone said or did to me and no matter how they said it or why, how I would respond was totally up to me and whatever decision I would make would, I would be help totally accountable.

REFLECTIONS

I didn't let anything get past me. I spoke up about everything and defended everybody like I was getting paid. I said everything that came to my head without caring what somebody thought. Write down examples about that moment when you decided that you had to say something. Was it a life or death situation? Did your words hurt someone else?

Did you feel better after you spoke up?

_____

_____

_____

_____

_____

_____

_____

_____

_____

_____

_____

Do you regret your decision about speaking up? Would you have done something differently or did you feel that was the only way to respond?

_____

_____

_____

To Be or Not To Be, Quiet

Have you ever had a moment when you were in the middle of a conversation that was not going your way and to "fix" the situation, you decided to just Shut Up, I mean, you wouldn't say one word? Yeah, you remember. Or maybe you had some information that would have been extremely helpful to someone else but you chose to keep quiet and not help or share because, you were angry with them for some reason, or you recalled a time that they pissed you off and you wanted to teach then a lesson, you know the comment, "That's what you get", ever used that one before? Or maybe you didn't say it but you were thinking it. Yep, you were being Petty.

As I started to develop relationships as an adult whether it be friends' co-workers or even boyfriends etc. Conversations became very different and the power of my voice would change. I did have more control over what I chose to say and how, but at the same time, the tests and challenges became more complicated. When you are grown,

42

you tend to think that you can say whatever you want to say and you say, but is that true? Do you think you have more responsibility or less when you become an adult? Although you are in charge of self, you are now leader of many, whether it be children, employees, family or whoever, so the way you behave and what you say will be influencing how younger people learn to communicate. Just something for you to keep in mind.

To be honest, this time in my life was truly one of the most challenging in relation to communication and knowing when, how and why to speak up. As an adult, you interact with a lot more people and now what you say or not say can affect every aspect of your life. Your friendships, your job and even your relationships can be affected in an instant based on what you say. Now for a little transparency. I was going through a time in my life when I was a new wife, with a blended family, and everybody didn't always get a long and on some level, may not have even liked each other. Blended families can be extremely difficult at times. This was a time in my life where the Power of Shut up would truly come into play. My whole perception of what it meant to Shut Up was about to be tested. This chapter will share some things I learned about me more so than anyone else.

I remember that there was a time in my marriage when arguing was almost a daily thing. We were challenged with trying to figure out how to be step-parents to all of our children who weren't necessarily too crazy about the idea of us being together as well as feelings of disrespect in our roles as husband and wife dealing with family, friends, exes, etc. Life was tough during this time and tensions were running high. Everyone was trying to watch what they would say, hold back to avoid arguments or misunderstanding while trying to figure out the best time to voice our concerns and feelings in hopes that things would change. That's not asking for too much right?

For myself, I felt really concerned about not wanted to come off as the evil stepmother, so I was extra cautious about speaking up. I spent a lot of time trying to please everyone and make sure everyone was happy. That's possible right? Of course, it is. We all know how impossible that is, but it never stops us from trying. I just knew I would be able to figure this one out and rule the world, lol. Initially I would stay quiet, trying to keep the peace, trying to be understanding about everyone's feelings, but that would prove to be extremely difficult.

Disrespect was one of my biggest pet peeves as an adult and parent. To allow or ignore it on any level made me feel like I was defying who I was as a woman, as a person. I had to find a way to approach the conversation without starting an argument, but it was turning out to be something I wasn't very good at. First, I was approaching this thing all wrong and didn't even realize it. I would start to bring up just about everything that was going on that I felt wasn't right. For example; I would fuss, almost daily sometimes, that the kids didn't do what I asked them to do, or when I asked them to do it, and almost regularly produced an argument with my husband. Words would get harsh, sometimes down right mean. Although there are certain words, we have NEVER used with each other in a argument, we aren't perfect so we threw a few harsh ones around every now and then. (Disclaimer: Name-calling is a No-No in our marriage) but we did pretty good at arguing without it. The problem that I started to realize I had was I was constantly bringing up the same issues, repeatedly. Not that they were not legitimate, but I became a broken record, running in the same groove without movement. When you are constantly saying the same thing repeatedly you will most definitely lose all the power in your words. Believe me, I learned the hard way. I know as a mom and wife we think that we must constantly reiterate what we are saying because none of them ever listen to us, especially the first time, I get it, but the fact is that the more we repeat, the less they hear, so we have to be mindful.

Well, he had his style of arguing and I had mine. See, I am a communicator by nature. I love to talk, work things out, you know, put it all out on the table, and he, let's just say, he is the opposite.....which left me wide open most of time and it left opportunity for him to play that shut 'em down by Shutting Up game.

Yes, that was the game that hubby was great at, but I was horrible at it. He had discovered "my" button and he also discovered that he knew how to push it. He used his Power of Shut Up in a way that drove me crazy. I can share this with you all because we have grown pass this. I chose this example to show you how the power can be misused and misunderstood, but you can absolutely grow from it. Not to say that knowing this will always help you to avoid the game, and certainly not every time, but making you aware is sometimes a lot of the battle.

Because I had a need to express myself and share my feelings (with little to no limits or acknowledgement of time) lol, as mentioned in the previous chapter, I was persistent and demanding almost all the time that everything needed to be discussed RIGHT NOW, while he on the other hand, was on team NOT NOW! Nothing needed to be discussed right away or even at all for him most of the time. We were all over the place. What a mess, right? YES, it was, and it was a continuous struggle of power for us. We were using our power in very different ways that never seemed to mesh. The funny thing was that we both wanted the same thing, which was resolve and peace, but because we had not learned how to communicate more effectively with each other and know when we could both talk and receive each other's views, we stayed in a constant struggle.

His thoughts - I changed the game and took control of the situation. Made it seem like an intellectual move by saying/suggesting things like, "I don't have time to argue with you" or "I'm tired of talking about this over and over again" or sometimes "this is petty, just let it go!"

Her thoughts - I changed the game and took control of the situation, giving the impression that I was being the more responsible one it this argument by saying/suggesting things like, "We need to talk about this now because it is unhealthy to let things fester" Stop holding things in and just talk to me" or even, "you are being immature and childish by not talking. Even setting limits on how long the silence should be tolerated.

Does any of this sound familiar? Sure, it does. There are probably various scenarios that we could share but I am sure you get what I am saying, we were both mis-using the power! We were trying to control the situation so that things would go OUR way, meaning, he didn't want to talk so his way worked, and I did so my way worked, but guess what? Nothing was ever accomplished because we were both busy being RIGHT and had not learned how and when to use the Power of Shut Up!

Lessons Learned

First of all, let's make things clear. Everything does not have to be discussed RIGHT NOW! I will open and honestly admit that, there is absolutely a time and place for everything to be discussed and just because you like to talk, doesn't mean that someone else must talk.

In addition to that, remember that every time someone wants to talk or opens their mouth to speak does not mean that they are arguing, nor is every conversation that does not go your way to be considered as a meaningless and unnecessary discussion. I am in no way suggesting that coming to this conclusion was an overnight thing but realizing and then accepting little things like this really helped us in the way we decided to even have a conversation about anything. The key was that we needed to make sure it was addressed, but how we did it needed a strategy. Hopefully "The Power of Shut Up" will give you that strategy.

There have been so many times when sarcasm would jump straight to my lips within seconds and jumped right out of mouth the very next second and I said things that I knew would hurt or knew would not be nice, etc. but because I was aware of how powerful the tongue was but unaware of the control I didn't have over it, I said it and then yes, a lot of times, I regretted it. One thing that I started to figure out in addition to when to speak was to pay attention to my intentions when speaking as well.

- What are we trying to achieve when we Speak Up or "Shut Up"?
- Am I in "payback status?
- Am I trying to teach someone a lesson?
- What is my temperament when responding to someone or something?
- Am I angry?
- Am I hurt?
- Will speaking up make the situation better or worse?
- Will the relationship grow from the conversation?
- Will we lose something if we don't have this conversation?

Check this out, how many times have you been in a situation where you are driving in traffic, and low and behold, someone cuts you off! Now here is a test that most have probably failed many times. We start cussing, fussing and giving hand gestures, right away, right? Say it ain't true. We are offended instantly that they would jump in front of us, they could have possibly caused an accident or even just got somewhere before us because we have been waiting in line for a minute. But let's assess the situation really quick. Giving the way the world is now-a days, all those above reactions could have major consequences. People are dying everyday responding to everyday occurrences that seem minor and silly at first but turn into deadly and harmful situations immediately. Sometimes shutting up can be considered a matter of life or death, #realtalk. If we just took a few minutes to decide whether it's worth it or not, we would still speak up, or would the result be to just shut up and go home to spend another wonderful day with your family, or your wife, or your parents? Would you gain some peace or lose it? I truly suggest that we start to learn how to take just one moment to think about it. Learning how to take just one minute to think about "what might happen if" could change the outcome of a bad situation into a resolved situation.

Let me share with you just how much peace I found when I decided not to engage every argument or attend or accept the invitation to every "Petty Party" and keep my mouth shut! Now don't get me wrong, there will be times when you need to speak up and say something, but what I found was that when I took that minute to think "What am I going to accomplish by venting, or yelling and fussing?" I usually came up with the decision that it wasn't even worth the energy I would have to use to attend, so most of the time, I decided not to speak up and after another few minutes of silence, I was over the moment. It really works sometimes, try it, you might like it!

I personally believe that we hold on to things that don't really matter too much and too long most of the time. We spend so much of our energy responding to things that don't change our circumstances or the world, won't make a difference or matter once you leave the situation or will only cause you pain and make you feel empty inside. We have allowed others, or given them the power to drain our energy, or what some may say, "Steal your Joy"! My advice, Don't do it!

What I have found is that it is extremely easy to be petty, but I want to encourage you to burn those petty files and start replacing them with peace. You may be adding years to your life by keeping that stress down, seriously. When you learn to ignore those things that don't matter just a few minutes later, you truly do find a peace within that allows you to shake it off easier the next time.

Try these steps that I follow (most of the time) that helped me to learn how to redirect my energy when something petty happens and you need to decide quickly on how to respond.

When that moment arrives, before speaking verbally:

> Step 1: THINK about WHY you are responding? Is it because you need to, or you just want to? If you need to, decide what will be accomplished when you do as well as assess who you are getting ready to respond to.

> Step 2: If you just want to and there is nothing of substance as far a reason beyond that, LET IT GO!

Here is some food for thought!

One thing that changed my knee-jerk responses to people was that although I can certainly hold my own whenever necessary, there are a whole lot more people out there that are crazier than me!

Life is too short and to keep things in perspective, I will take an educated guess that your #PettyFiles are taking up a whole lot of space that you could be replacing with smiles and laughter and a peace of mind.

REFLECTIONS

I let my pride get in the way many times, How about you? Did you ever respond to any given situation out of pettiness? Did you say something or respond harshly to someone only because you wanted to pay them back for doing you wrong or mistreating you?

_____
_____
_____
_____
_____
_____
_____
_____
_____
_____
_____
_____
_____
_____
_____
_____
_____
_____

Do you know their intentions when you responded to them or did you assume and then react?

_____
_____

Every Thought Does Not Have To Be Spoken

I know, I know, …there are some real struggles and challenges when it comes to speaking up to defend what's right and things like that. and the reality is that we aren't perfect, so there will always be times when you try to ignore the mess and you just can't. We think we must speak up for ourselves when someone disrespects us, and we are absolutely free to exercise our right to free speech. I know that we need to exercise our right (to not speak too) at times, yes, but, let me be clear about something, shutting up doesn't mean that you have no voice, not at all! Everything does not have to be verbal and there is a lot said in silence, believe me. I spoke in my loudest voice was when I said nothing at all.

There will be times in life when you are being called out your name, verbally assaulted, threatened, ridiculed, etc., and the 1st thing you want to do is what? Cuss somebody out. I get it…Been there, done that! But in this chapter, I want to share the ways I learned how being silent or "shutting up" spoke louder than any words that I could have ever come out of my mouth. Learning to shut my mouth sometimes actually taught me to hear what was being said or "communicated", before reacting or responding, and sometimes that moment of listening made it abundantly clear that a response was not even necessary. I had to learn to listen intentionally and speak purposefully. I learned that sometimes I said more by not saying anything.

When I tell you, I had to have the last word, oh my goodness. I didn't let anything slip, pass, fly by me. When you have felt like you have never been able to speak up without being judged or chastised or made fun of and you have had enough, things change and you start smelling yourself, (as my momma would say)! I always used that fact that I felt I was being disrespected as my reason (or excuse) for a #snapback. I wasn't going to let anyone disrespect me or mine, so I felt the need to LET YOU KNOW!

I remember being out to dinner with my husband and I recall that I commented on something that happened while we were there that made me angry, ok, I said transparency, pissed me off. It might have been bad service or the way someone had spoken to me, can't recall exactly what, but I know that I was complaining about something.

I felt like I needed to let them know that what they did was not acceptable, so I was ready to say something. While I was waiting for them to return so I could let them have a piece of my mind, my husband turned to me and said, "You know you don't have to say everything that comes to your head", and my response was, "Why?". Why couldn't I just address the situation so that I would not happen again. I was totally confused by his comment initially, never-mind the fact that this was coming from my husband, who I had perceived as someone who NEVER said much of anything to people when they did something wrong and always gave a pass to folks for bad behavior. Some of the women may be able to relate to me but I always felt that in the area of communication, I was an A+ student and he was a C-, lol. It was almost as if I thought that I would explode or something if I did not speak up when there was a mess up.

How was someone going to know what they did wrong if I didn't let them know, right? WRONG!

During that short conversation while waiting for the waiter/waitress to return, I came to some serious revelations about Shutting Up! He was right. (Don't tell him though, I will never live it down). What he didn't realize at that moment is that even though I thought that he wasn't such a great communicator, he was teaching me a few things about the power of the tongue and patience. I had always admired the fact they he was always calmer than me, rarely getting flustered or all worked up and was just over all more pleasant at times, despite a bad situation. But at the same time, I thought his was just too nice sometimes, letting everything go because he was just avoiding confrontation. But what was I gaining? I was losing my cool, pissed off, carrying a major attitude and most of the time, a good portion of my day was ruined or greatly disrupted and for what? It wasn't that I thought he had necessarily figured out this communication thing and I didn't. The fact was that most of the time, he felt the same way I did about what was going on, but the difference was that we expressed things in a different way. I was boisterous about everything while he remained calm and rarely spoke up. But what I did start to notice was intent and consequence. He seemed to be responding based on the future consequences while I was responding based on my present situation. Neither was necessarily wrong, they were different. And they were viewed differently by others. He was seen as calm and understanding while I came across as difficult and mean. What I was realizing was that although you can feel the same way about things, how you respond can sometimes, well, a lot of times, dictate how people will receive and respond and view you.

Keeping things in perspective, the fact was that the service was not so great. We both knew that, but where I felt the need to let them know (the waiter/waitress), my husband felt like it was not necessary. Is there a right or wrong way to do it? Some would say absolutely but I will challenge you and say maybe not. The real question to me became, did your response get you the desired outcome? Did the service get better, or did it stay the same or get worse by "letting them know"? Did they feel attacked, insulted and get angry or did they embrace the observations, apologize or even provide an explanation? Think about it. What do you think?

_____

_____

_____

_____

_____

_____

_____

_____

I was learning that you will be invited to all kinds of disagreements, arguments and, depending on the age or sex, fights, but, you DO NOT have to accept the invite. You can decline the invitation and not attend but it is your decision. You have to decide if accepting the invite will prove to be a great experience that moves everyone involved forward or if it will be an experience that causes everyone to step back. It made me reflect to my middle school years and that incident on the school bus. I remembered the judgement, I remembered the misunderstanding, but I also remembered the fact that it was also perception based on communication.

Yes, you have a voice, and yes, you are supposed to use it, but the purpose of this book is to show you how to use it in a productive and meaningful way.

REFLECTIONS

Must you respond to Everything? Shut Up Already! Why do you feel like you have to respond to everything? What do you think will happen if you don't respond?

_____

_____

_____

_____

_____

_____

_____

_____

_____

_____

_____

_____

_____

_____

_____

_____

_____

_____

_____

_____

_____

_____

_____

_____

_____

It's Healthy To Shut Up Sometimes

I know some of you won't believe me but shutting up proved to be beneficial to my health. I know, I know, you are probably thinking, Yeah right?

In this chapter I will share with you how running my mouth and shutting my mouth affected my health. I didn't quite understand or realize how what I said out of my mouth would affect me, but I finally get it.

Several years ago, I experienced something that would affect the rest my life in a major way. I learned some things through my journey that would make me look at life, love, relationships and everything in a very different way. Several years ago, I was going through a very difficult time in my life. Although married with children, surrounded by some great friends, great job and some family that truly cared about me, I wasn't finding any peace in my life. There were outside people and things that I had allowed to control my space by keeping me irritated and angry most of my days. Let me be very transparent, in life you will come across situations that you can't control and you either have to find a way to get through or walk away.

Driving home one day after grabbing a bite to eat, I was having a venting session with my girlfriend on my phone, (hands-free, of course) about something that was pissing my off. We all have had those conversations where you are cussing and fussing, practically yelling in the phone to your friend about things that are getting on your nerves. And a lot of times, it's a conversation/venting session that has occurred many times before. For me, this was one of those days.

I was driving along practically yelling in the phone about something that I had talked about probably 50 times before, so it was nothing new or different. I am sure my girlfriend was probably like, "Here we go again", lol, but like we do for our friends, we listen and support! Not realizing how worked up and heated I was, in the middle of my sentence as I started to swallow, and suddenly, I couldn't! It seemed to be a struggle to do take a swallow. It was as if something was blocking my throat and I couldn't swallow, which in turn made me think that breathing was becoming difficult. I can't remember word for word, but the minute it happened, I vaguely remember saying something to my girlfriend to the effect of, "Girl, let me call you back," Let me remind you, because I wasn't sure what was going on, I didn't quite let on to her how scared I was but I was TERRIFIED! Now don't hold me to the exact words because it truly is a blur but what I do know is that something had happened, and I was now in panic mode. Just one minute from my house, I made my way into the house totally unhinged but still maintaining a sense of composure, trying to figure out what was happening to me. I went in the house and immediately called my husband.

All I can remember saying to him was that something wasn't right, and I was feeling like I couldn't breathe and that I was going to die. Now, I know you are thinking that is drastic, but it was exactly what I felt at that moment. I could not seem to process anything outside of the thought that I was dying, and my air supply was becoming less and less. The one thing that I remember repeating repeatedly was, "I'm not going to make it, I'm not going to make it, I think I am going to Die!"

Now, let me explain something to you, I was truly under the impression that my breathing was limited, and because this whole series of events started because I couldn't swallow normally, I thought that I was choking. For some reason I thought that if my mouth stays dry, I was going to continue to choke. Can you imagine the feeling you would experience if you swallowed a whole spoonful of peanut butter and it wouldn't go down, that's how I felt?

I grabbed a 2-liter, yes, a 2-liter of Rock Creek soda, the red flavor, fruit punch, right? It's amazing what information your mind will hold and how it processes things under extreme stress. Anyway, I grabbed the soda bottle and a small cup on the way out the door, why? Because in my mind I needed to keep my palette wet to make it easier to swallow. Minutes later we arrived and went in to the front desk, 2-liter soda and cup in hand and anxious, ready to see somebody and quick. I explained to the nurse that I couldn't breath and really needed to see a doctor in a hurry. Because no one was understanding why this was an emergency, mainly because I didn't know myself what I was feeling, there was almost no understanding or compassion.

For the life of me I can't remember her name, but I do remember a petite lady, medium length blonde haired woman, wearing a white nurse's jacket come to the doorway, you know the one that stays locked and can't be opened unless you are buzzed in, and say, "Come with me", which were the best words you could have ever said to me. The next thing she said to me was, "You are going to be alright". All my vitals were fine and based on the machines, my breathing was fine, my heart was fine and I was ok, and yet I was still feeling like I was going to die. WHY? I was having a panic attack!

An x-ray and shot later to confirm everything else were good and to relax my nerves, which didn't work by the way, my husband was taking me home and still stressed because I was still not feeling great and struggling to swallow. That evening at home was probably the worst night of my life, I paced the floor down to the wood, I struggled with swallowing all night and I got absolutely NO SLEEP. I laid down and then would sit right back up continuously trying to relax, feeling like laying down was blocking my airways too. I even suggested to my husband that we head back to the doctor/emergency room because things were no better than they were when I left. But I stressed myself, and him, out so bad that eventually I got so exhausted that I finally feel asleep and got some rest. But that was short lived because as soon as I woke up, i picked up right where I had left off and was feeling a lot of anxiety and again, struggling with swallowing. I didn't want to eat or drink anything because I choked on everything trying to manage my swallowing.

My life was changing right before my eyes and I couldn't seem to control it. Being very strong an independent most of my life, this was traumatizing on so many levels to me. I was losing control of my entire life and I didn't like it at all. I became everything that I wasn't, dependent, angry, needy and scared all the time. My self-confidence, my trust, my feeling of comfort, everything, was gone. I didn't want to be home alone, but I also didn't want to talk to friends, and family conversations were limited to my mom. I also didn't want to go anywhere, because I had lost trust in my instincts and had already had one incident where I decided to venture out and take my son somewhere, but not even ½ a mile from our driveway, the anxiety kicked in and I no longer trusted myself on the road, and I definitely was going to be able to get on a highway or any busy roads, so we headed back home and he had to call someone to pick him up. My emotions were all over the place because I truly felt like I had lost any control I thought I had over my entire life, and on top of that, I felt like I was a burden to husband and couldn't explain what was happening to me, and if I was frustrating about what was happening to me, I know he had to be frustrated.

I had started to isolate myself and interacted with those who literally lived in my house. I hated when my husband left for work because I didn't like being left alone but there wasn't a lot of conversation because when you talk you swallow and that was something that I had seemed to not do very well. I kept my conversations when people called to check on me at a real minimum. I didn't say much and sometimes even rushed people off the phone, not because I was being ungrateful, not at all, but because I was literally terrified that I would choke if I talked to much and when you

66

choke, your cut off your breathing and that translated to death in my mind, and like I said, I didn't want to die!

It is a stressful situation when all the tests are showing that things are great, but your body and mind are telling you that something is wrong. But I was about to get some clarity that would help me start to put things in perspective and make better sense about what was really going on. Some of you reading this may start to figure some of this out too and others might be learning something brand new. It was the moment I had been waiting for since all this happened. The results were in, and based on my barium test, I had GERD and Acid Reflux! Maybe that explained a lot and maybe it didn't. I was finally getting some clarity on my situation, at least technically speaking, but now I had to figure out what all this would mean to me and how I would proceed with this information, and obviously this was not a good thing.

Let me say this, the Lord works in mysterious ways. Sometimes he will allow things to happen in your life that help you to put things in perspective and to help you to focus on what is important. You tend to listen and hear more when you aren't talking and SHUT UP! Think about it.

The more I found out about why this happened to me physically, the more I became focused mentally on what I needed to do to make sure I didn't have those episodes again. The feelings of anxiety had started to lessen and I was regaining my confidence in general, things were looking up. I won't share all the details here, but I will say that as I started to learn more about my body and what I should be eating to avoid these choking bouts, I completely cleaned out my whole system.

See, your body holds all types of toxins and when you start to actually eat right and clean your system of all those toxins, it's actually a very painful experience, at least it was for me it was, but on the plus side I had started to gain energy and focus. It is sometimes hard to explain when I have shared this story before, but it was as if I had put on some brand-new glasses. I was seeing life in a brand-new way.

When I took a moment to reflect on all that had happened and how everything started, one thing came to mind that relates directly to the Power of Shut Up! I was literally running my mouth and fussing about all things that were pissing me off, making me mad and making me feel bad about people who had no control over my life, and in an instant, everything was changing. I stopped talking, fussing, complaining, eating, drinking, and speaking!

Remember I told you that I stopped communicating with everyone. I talked to a chosen few, and then my communication with them was extremely limited, but not only that, I was also reacting very differently to the energy in conversations and even the subject matter that was discussed. In that moment when it all started, although some of things I was complaining about were legitimate issues, the energy that I was using to discuss them was very toxic, negative, and frankly unproductive and it was time to Shut Up. It was like my mind, body and soul could no longer process nonsense and negativity. I was spending too much time focusing on what others were doing wrong and not enough time focusing on what I needed to be doing to press forward and live my life right.

This event that had happened in my life was one of the most eye-opening moments for me in my life. To this day, I will always remember in detail how everything happened and the many many lessons that I learned from it. I learned, in the strangest way possible, to shut my mouth and do something different. What I was saying out of my mouth had direct consequences to my health. It was true!

I started to change my whole perspective on life in ways that changed the way I did a lot of things in my life. You know that road rage that everyone has heard of, and probably most of us have experienced in one way or another, I had those moments too, until this happened to me. I stopped rushing to my next destination, fussing at the driver in front of me that was driving to slow, or the one that was driving too close behind me and started taking my time, you know why? for several reasons, like, Life is way too short! Think about this:

Sometimes God has you late to your destination because there is danger ahead or someone needs you.

- An accident was on the route you would take
- You would have missed an emergency call
- You would have left your wallet if you didn't slow down

Sometimes someone is driving slow in front of you because they are being cautious because:

- There may be nails on the road ahead
- There is a big pot hole in the middle of the road
- The police are up ahead
- Sometimes someone may be headed to the emergency room
- Someone is having a baby
- Someone is sick
- Someone has been in an accident

- Someone is needing help roadside

Sometimes someone is having a bad day that has nothing to do with you and they are simply taking it out on the world, like:

- they lost a loved one
- they lost their job
- they had an argument with a spouse
- they are simply having a bad day

Let me say this, God has a way of showing up in your life at the right time. And whatever he needs to do to get your attention, he is going to do it in a way that makes you stand up and take notice. God was trying to let me know that enough was enough and that needed to change some things in my life, and quick. I was spending so much time allowing people to control my peace and it was starting to affect me mentally and physically. I was unhappy more than I was happy because I was focused on everything and everyone else but me, but things were taking a big turn, for the better. The scare that I had just experienced in my life would change me forever. I approached life in a very different and positive way and even changed that way I spoke and interacted with people. I was calmer and more forgiving, and really learned how to let go of things that I had absolutely no control over. I stopped addressing every little thing and only gave energy to those things where it was necessary, and in most cases, it wasn't necessary at all. I was experiencing life in a brand-new way. I changed some of my daily practices as I started to gain a greater awareness of the power of words. I started to do things that truly helped me to live a more peaceful life. How you speak to yourself on a regular basis is one of the most important things you can do for yourself:

- ❖ I practiced writing and speaking positive affirmation
- ❖ I journaled when I became frustrated
- ❖ When I encountered a challenging situation, i would literally count to ten slowly to relax
- ❖ I watch shows and movies that would stress me through fear or anger less and less
- ❖ I learned to ignore people who I felt were trying to pull me out of my character
- ❖ I wrote down a bucket list of the things that I wanted to do throughout my life and set limits on many of them to help me to be accountable

These were just a few of the things that I would start to do to help me to clear my mind of all things negative. Now, these all may not work for you, but try a few and see how it works for you. When I started to focus on my goals and dreams, I had less time to criticize, judge or tolerate anyone else's issues.

REFLECTIONS

Must you respond to Everything? Shut Up Already
Why do you feel like you have to respond to everything?
What do you think will happen if you don't respond?

_____

_____

_____

_____

_____

_____

_____

_____

_____

_____

_____

_____

_____

_____

_____

_____

_____

_____

_____

_____

_____

_____

_____

Don't Block Your Blessings

The art of silent speaking is truly a craft. I know you are probably asking, "How in the heck can you be heard if you are silent. In this chapter I will share several "WOW" moments that helped me to not only understand that it could be done, but I also started to learn, slowly I might add, how to still be heard. I fought the idea of "Shutting Up" when I was first thinking about writing this book because my voice was my everything to me. My voice had become my outlet, my strength, my power, and the suggestion that I need to be quiet or Shut Up was not only offensive but was asking me to not have a voice, an opinion, an existence. I had worked so hard to break out of my silence in so many instances growing up that the suggestion that I was supposed to give it up wsa beyond unacceptable.

It was imperative that I speak because most of my life I had missed those opportunities when I probably needed to speak up and now that I had found my voice, I did NOT want to give it up. I truly felt that if I didn't speak up that I would never get the respect that I deserved that I had never seemed to get before. Why would I go back to a time when people would try to take advantage of me or not value me as a person. Not going to happen. I had been quiet for so long that the thought of being silent was terrifying! I would NEVER allow anyone to take away my voice or tell me to shut up because that was the only way I could stop people from making me feel like I didn't matter or that what I had to say or what I was thinking meant nothing. I was fighting inside for years, struggling with my inner being about feeling weak, like a punk, why was a scared to say what I was thinking? And now that I had conquered that, I was supposed to embrace some Shut Up power, it seems silly, but the thought was traumatizing.

There was a moment where I was frustrated with what was going on in my marriage. We loved each other but our surroundings were not in sync with our union. The blended family thing was taking its toll on the both of us and because there are no rules to how blended families are supposed to work, we were winging it. Yes, we got it right sometimes, but the reality was, because the children were not speaking up, ironically as I didn't as a child as well, we didn't really know how they truly felt and we all know that when you hold things in verbally, sometimes it comes out in your actions. I was busy trying to be that awesome step-mom that was fun and inclusive, and my husband was trying to make sure that everyone was getting along and that everyone was happy. That was a lot and some of it was nearly impossible. But the issues didn't stop there, there were also those outside influences that we had to deal with that made things difficult. Past relationships, in-laws, friends, family, and just life in general was changing and what worked before was missing its mark in our current situation.

Trying to figure out how to take your world and someone else's world with all the experiences, old relationships, attitudes, hurts, disappointments, expectations, old habits etc. and blend them into one happy place was extremely challenging at times. I spent the early part of my marriage trying to stay quiet and go along with the program, because who wants to make things difficult and be seen as the difficult one, not me. But to be honest, that is exactly what I was doing. I didn't want my in-laws, the children or even my husband to think bad of me but because I had to say something about everything, I was getting exactly what I didn't want. Now, this doesn't mean that I was wrong in what I felt or that the things that were happening were not right or nice but somehow, I was turning into the bad guy in the situation. I was at a point in my life where speaking up was necessary and I needed to say it, but it wasn't making me happy afterwards. I was miserable after getting things off my chest. My thoughts were, how would we be able to fix the problems and get through the drama if I didn't point them out, right? Maybe, maybe not.

Picture this, it seemed like almost daily I was bringing something up that somebody did, said or implied that made me feel disrespected, hurt or sometimes down right mean. I mean I spoke up so much about each and every little thing that I was actually tired of hearing myself talk, no lie. I was annoyed with my own voice at times. But I really had a hang up about the fact that if I ignored it or didn't make it plain, I was doing myself an injustice, any everyone else for that matter. How would my issues be heard? How would they know that what they were doing was hurting me? Maybe some of you can relate to this. And to add to the drama, I didn't just say it once, I said it repeatedly and I was saying loud, sometimes upset, sometimes firm but always SAYING IT!

I would have conversations with my mom, friends, etc. about my frustrations with everything, many times in tears. Why was I the bad guy? Why was I viewed as the Mean one? Why am I wrong? And then I remember the words my mother said to me and I had a "WOW" moment, "Stop saying it so people can see it for themselves". Wait, how does that work. My arrogance about the situation allowed me to believe that I was the ONLY one who could see what was happening. ONLY I could articulate what was going on, so how could I not say it and be understood. But, guess what, she was right on point. I was blocking my own blessings. I wasn't finding peace because I wasn't giving any! Do you find yourself constantly complaining about things, like:

➢ The kids didn't do the dishes again,
➢ Your husband didn't finish that project he has been working on,
➢ Your friend didn't return your call again,
➢ You were left a hold on a call for too long,

➢ Someone cut you off on the road rushing,
➢ Nobody is supporting you.

And the list can go on and on. Have there been times when you can actually hear yourself fussing in your head because you have done it so much. That was one of those moments when I realized, I need to Shut Up! You come to a moment when you realize that what you are doing or what you are saying is not working and it's time to do something different. Your goal is to get through any difficult situation better or more knowledgeable than when you started. And of course, the main goal is to bring peace to the situation and hopefully resolution. Here are a few things I want you to think about before you speak:

> Check your intentions for saying it!
> Check your surroundings when you say it!
> Check the necessity to say it!
> Check what you will gain or lose from saying it!
> Check your tone when you do say! (If you decide to say it!)

REFLECTIONS

Embracing the Power of Shut Up

I tell you what, it took me damn near 45 years or more to understand the Power of shutting up and keeping my mouth closed. And it wasn't an easy lesson. I can truly admit that sometimes I should have kept my mouth shut, but instead I ran my mouth right into some mess. I had to learn that silence can be just as loud as speaking. I would sometimes, (a lot of times) share my feeling, thoughts and ideas would others and they were offended in some way but what I said or how I said it and didn't receive it well. I was accused at times for being insensitive, or harsh, and even confrontational. Now, to be honest, at times that was probably very true but for very different reasons that they knew. I was convinced that speaking my mind and "Keeping it REAL" was always the way to go and that I was doing myself and others and injustice but holding it in but, that was absolutely an excuse most of the time to simply get my point across. I am here to tell you that "Keeping it REAL" is relative. What do I mean when I say that? I will tell you. Keeping it REAL only means that you are speaking from YOUR experience and opinion of what is correct and if that is the case, we all are Keeping it REAL! There is no safety in speaking from that space. You will walk into drama and confusion 90% of the time working from that direction. I started to feel like when people say that, it is more of a disclaimer before they give you their opinion on YOUR situation which a lot of times was not even invited or requested.

I had to learn to be humble to the fact that what I share with others regarding any situation on what I would do or what I would say or even how I would feel has nothing to with you and EVERYTHING to do with me. I constantly tell myself......

➢ Did somebody ask you for YOUR opinion?
➢ Did somebody ask you what you think THEY should do?
➢ Did someone share information and tell you to gather all they business and then give your ideas on what is going on in THEIR life?

We truly need to learn to think first and speak last or sometimes NEVER! Really, NEVER is sometimes the answer.

At some point or another we all think that we know more than many about a situation that we have gone through or experienced in life. We give advice and speak with absolute authority and will challenge anyone that doesn't agree, but we must remember that we are speaking from our perspective, and the reality is that there are many, many perspectives to consider. After experiencing so many things in life that changed my feelings on how to express myself, when to speak up and when not to, I have gained so much peace in finally understand that there may be a method to this madness.

It was stressing me out in a major way to feel like I had to address every issue that I didn't see the same way as others, every person that I did not agree with, every situation where I felt disrespected and so on. The energy that I used to accept every argument and defend every stance was draining and honestly probably taking years off my life! I was stealing my own joy for years. I learned that life is too short and that I needed to change my focus in life. Instead of spending most of my time defending my position in the world, I started to just live and let my actions speak for themselves. I stopped feeling like it was necessary to prove everything to everybody.

The first step to moving in the right direction is acknowledging that you might have been able to do things in a different way. Second step is to accept that fact that it didn't make you feel good to say what you said anyway, in fact, you actually felt bad many times after reacting with your words. Yeah, you said what to wanted to say and they heard you, but, did it make you feel better for getting it off your chest? A lot of times the answer is no!

This is the part of my journey when I had to eat some humble pie. All the excuses and issues I used that allowed me to justify why I needed to say something all the time, why I needed to tell 'em how it was all the time, or the ripe old saying, how I always felt the need to keep it REAL! I started to understand that all the things you say are ONLY your perspective and you have to keep that in mind when you speak. I learned that, Yes, I have an opinion, but so does everyone else and what seems necessary to me may not to someone else. Take that minute to evaluate your intentions before speaking, Think About It! You may save yourself from an unwanted argument or even losing someone. Words have tremendous power and if you don't start to understand the power of words, you will continue to use them inappropriately. Now, do I get it right all the time? No. This is absolutely a work in progress for a lifetime. These are lessons that I learned that truly lifted some heavy feelings of hurt and stress on my life.

I started to understand that the less I said the more others heard. Does that make sense? I know it sounds backwards but it's true. When I stopped pointing out what others were doing and saying that wasn't right, it exposed them on so many levels. The people I was trying to expose the truth to were able to see it for themselves when I shut my mouth.

I always thought that I had to show somebody what was going on, but the reality was that I was blocking it. I was making it difficult for them to see because sometimes when you are sharing information and telling what you see to be true, people become defensive and even embarrassed sometimes that it wasn't clear to them. And understand this, shutting up does not mean that you were wrong, your feelings aren't valid or anything like that. It means that you are comfortable in your truth. I have to admit, humbling myself to a point where I didn't say anything sometimes was the hardest part of all of this for me. I was not an easy process for me because a lot of my issues about everyone else until I realized that how I felt everyday was totally up to me. I was responsible for my happiness.

REFLECTIONS

Have you ever spoke up about something only to find out that you misunderstood what was being said and you had to take back those words? Share

_____

_____

_____

_____

_____

_____

_____

_____

_____

_____

Let's be very honest – Did you go back and apologize? Did you actually take ownership for speaking to quickly?

Reminder: Thinking before you speak may save you a few apologies 😊

_____

_____

_____

_____

_____

_____

_____

_____

The Power of Shut Up with Friends/Social Settings

Let me share a moment when I truly understood the power of shut up. Have you ever had a moment when you have had a falling out with a friend/family member or even a co-worker? We all have and we have all said things that we didn't mean or said things that we meant but didn't mean to say them that way, whatever the case we will always run across situations where we are not in a good space with someone.

I had a bad conversation with friends and we all left the conversation very upset. Unfortunately, I soon found out that the conversations and disagreements we had, made their way to Social Media. Not good right? My heart sank at that very moment. Anyone who knew me knew that I try my hardest not to air dirty laundry on Social Media! But here it was, smacking me in my face. Now it was not clear to most because that is the very reason, we use subliminal messages right? But the fact remained that I knew who and what it was in reference to and I also knew that others may know too.

What is your gut reaction in that moment? Yeah, I know, push back, say things that would hurt that person, tit for tat in full effect, I get it. In that moment after picking my heart up off the floor, broken in pieces of course, I had to decide how I was going to respond to this situation that had just pushed ALL my buttons. You will constantly be pushed in pulled to step outside of yourself and act out of your character based on someone else's actions BUT, it's that minute that you step back and think, If I responded in like, I would be doing the same thing that I absolutely despised, If I responded and no one actually knew that it was in reference to me or my situation, I have now put my name to the game right? All kinds of things go through your mind when you are challenged to react or not react to something.

- ➢ Is it worth it to respond at all?
- ➢ What will you accomplish once you respond?
- ➢ Do you care that you are now "NOT DOING YOU" because this is something you would never do?
- ➢ Are you trying to hurt someone else the same way they hurt you?

These are just a few examples of the questions you should ask yourself in that #fallback moment.

Fast forward, I had some decisions to make and need I say I felt that they needed to be made quickly because my anger and hurt were winning this battle between responding responsibly or not or whether even to respond at all.

See, like me, some of you may have a big Respect Chip that you wear on your shoulder and you can't even recall at time that you let anyone slide when you felt disrespected.

But let me give you something to ponder. I had to think about how responding would affect all that I have going on that was good in my life. The energy that I would be disrupting if I continued this behavior because remember, when you respond to someone doing something inappropriate, or wrong, you are continuing the behavior whether what they did was right or wrong.

I concluded, with the help of my insightful husband, that responded was unnecessary. Now I will be very transparent with you in this moment. This was one of the most difficult decisions I have ever made, and I was challenged with it daily for weeks. Yes, weeks of the same behavior, and the truth is, when you get strong enough to not respond, it will intensify the bad behavior of others at first. It would get worse before it ever got better.

I had to exercise strength in silence that was not normal for me. How could I just sit here and watch someone talk and taunt me and not say anything? Some would suggest that you were being weak or a punk right? That is how I felt initially as I watched.

Let me share with you what happened. The longer I stayed silent and ignored the comments and posts, the more empowered I became. It's TRUE! I was gaining strength mentally every time I Shut Up and said nothing. How could that be?

I was starting to understand what the Power of Shut Up was all about. After I got over the initial frustration and questioning my own character, I started to think about other things the truly matters to me, my family, my work, my businesses, etc. and my focus changed. Instead of giving all that energy to what wasn't serving me well, I was re-directing that energy to places that were thriving from the increased attention. Learning how to Shut Up was teaching me how to focus. The messages on Social Media didn't necessarily stop, but I looked at them differently now. They didn't bother me like they had done before. I could look at them, know they were about me and smile. What a feeling it was to have the strength to see something that I didn't like and not have to address it each time. This is not to say that there will be times when you must address something without question, but it does suggest that you do NOT have to accept every invitation to "Cease your Peace"!

It only takes a few minutes to think before you react. It can really make a difference in how you handle all kinds of challenges in life. Yes, I felt bad about what had transpired but I also made a conscious decision to decline the invitation to the #petty party.

REFLECTIONS

Have you ever spoke up about something only to find out that you misunderstood what was being said and you had to take back those words? Share

_____

_____

_____

_____

_____

_____

_____

_____

_____

_____

Let's be very honest – Did you go back and apologize? Did you take ownership for speaking to quickly?

Reminder: Thinking before you speak may save you a few apologies 😊

_____

_____

_____

_____

_____

_____

_____

_____

The Power of Shut Up on The Job

The Power of Shut-Up is awesome because once you start to embrace it, those two words never quite mean the same again, No really! Watch this, once you see Shutting up as a good thing that empowers you, it loses its power and you gain yours! Let me explain.

Daily we are challenged once we obtain our "Super Power" because what happens when you have something that's worth a lot? Other people who don't have it, or they want to take it from you. But that is not your problem, it's theirs. In life we all must work with people in our businesses, on our jobs or in our organizations that we don't necessarily like or get along with. That is just a fact of life. You have to understand that you become a target when you obtain something that sets you apart from the norm. You can be a target for good or bad and you will experience both, but you have to be ready. Hopefully this book will help you to be proactive in being ready to take on anything in a positive way that keeps you moving forward. And since we all need our jobs, learning this skill on the job is essential in my opinion.

In life we must learn to get along with people that we don't particularly care for whether we like it or not. When you have situations working with others and you just can't seem to get along, everything they do bothers you are you start to pick at all the things they do that annoy you. A lot of times you become very vocal about how you feel about them, how they did you wrong, how they messed up on a project, etc. and because you don't like them, you are more than anxious to spread the word, share the fail, or remind them of what they did. You sometimes even seem vindicated in putting the "Fail" or "Mishap" on blast because they irritate you to the core. Most of us have had moments like that in life and never thought about how those very words you spoke about another were more damning to you than to them. See, I believe that the more you speak ill of someone else, the more you block your own blessings.

I worked really hard to always do my best at everything I did in life and took major offense when others would suggest differently. Being the kind of person who went over and beyond and would assist anyone who needed it, and do whatever I could, I often felt unappreciated because it was many times not reciprocated. People didn't always do the same for me that I did for them. I always learned that you treat people the way you want to be treated but we all know that it doesn't always work out that way. Nope, sometimes not even close to that way but, you have to still work with that person, keep a smile on your face and be professional at all times because, You NEED your job. Being the kind of person who had grown into a space where I never had a problem with speaking up, I voiced my opinion often. I was more than happy to share with a friend on how unhappy I was with how I was being treated, how I didn't deserve it and how I didn't have to take it, all true right? But what was I getting out of it? How was what I was doing making my situation any better? Were things changing for me? The answers to most of those questions is probably NO.

I was exhausted, upset and guess what, non-productive most of the time and didn't even realize it. I realized that I was spending more time talking about my issues and less time doing something about it. My focus was off and I couldn't possibly be giving my best effort to whatever I was doing because I was distracted. I was talking too much. And most of the time, no one was listening, believe me, they weren't. Here is where the power of shut up comes into play.

Sometimes you have to let your actions speak louder than your words. People will talk about you whether it's the truth or not and it really doesn't matter what you are saying. Shut-Up and just let your skills speak for themselves. I discovered something very important when I started to close my mouth, I could hear even better. 1st thing I started to notice was the obvious, when I started talking less about the wrongs that were happening and noticed that I got more work done, go figure. But more importantly was that I my creativity was more acute and started to focus and I was producing better work because I had less distractions and the energy was focused on something positive. I am in no way suggesting this is easy, but you would be amazed what happens in your life in any situation when you simply Shut Up.

Now I will say this, you will have those moments when you vent all the time and then you get tired of getting nowhere so you stop, and then guess what?, the foolishness starts again, so you indulge in the drama and start venting all over again, but here is the plus to the pattern. It will be easier this time because you know the benefits of shutting up or (being quiet). Test it. Ask yourself some questions. How much work are you getting down while you are complaining, fussing over venting about the issue? Unless you are typing, editing, reading, meeting, or doing whatever your skill is while you vent, fuss and complain, my educated guess is, not much, if any. Be honest with yourself. While you are busy fussing about the issue, they are busy working. Think about it.

I was hurting myself and didn't even realize it. Remember, no one can see what you are doing because they are too busy trying to listen to what you are saying. Let your work speak for you. Rise above the mess and stop the stress. It's not worth it in the stream of things because anything that distracts you from the reason you are there in the first place is probably not worth your energy. I know you are trying to point out what is not right, but instead of talking about it with people who for the most part can't or won't relate because (it ain't them), find who can help, what the procedures are to get the assistance and then, GET BACK TO WORK! Your family will thank you 😊

REFLECTIONS

Have you ever spoke up about something only to find out that you misunderstood what was being said and you had to take back those words? Share

_____

_____

_____

_____

_____

_____

_____

_____

_____

Let's be very honest – Did you go back and apologize? Did you actually take ownership for speaking to quickly?

Reminder: Thinking before you speak may save you a few apologies 😊

_____

_____

_____

_____

_____

_____

_____

The Power of Shut Up in Relationships

This chapter should be a lot of fun for all my married couples and folks in relationships. But you have to be able to take some blows to the ego so Get Ready, Set & Go!

Ladies and Gentlemen, it's about to get real.

Now some of you may not agree with me and that is quite alright, but these are things that I personally learned that helped me to grow as a wife and a woman. The lessons I learned about shutting up in my marriage challenged me at my core but changed my marriage in a great way. It also proved to be one of the biggest lessons I learned out of all the lessons I embraced as a wife.

Some will be able to relate to the duo where one of you loves to talk and one doesn't. Typically, it's the wife who always wants to talk all the time and the husband who doesn't but there are exceptions to the rule so please apply to the action and not the gender. ☺

I learned the two sides of the Power of Shut Up within my marriage. See, my husband was a man a very few words, unless he was mad of course…lol, and I was a woman of many, so we both learned some lessons along the way that helped us to be better able to get along. Learning when to shut up brought us closer together, believe it or not. Like I have mentioned earlier in the book, I was always under the impression that if you had something on your mind, you need to let it be known. Well, that rule was proven to not be 100% true. There are times when you should shut up and let things take their course. I'll explain why.

My husband and I have been married for almost 9 years and we have been friends for over 30 so we have learned a lot about each other over the years but, when you get married, no matter how long you have known each other, things do change. Because you are with each other every moment of the day sometimes and your whole world includes this one person forever, you start to notice a whole lot more when you are married. Over the years you will start to notice all the things that bother you, annoy you and frankly, get on your last nerve, it's true and normal sometimes in my opinion, and we were no exception. But my husband, being the "non-talker" would hold his feelings in, while I was letting my spill all over the house. I pointed out everything that I noticed that wasn't to my liking. You know the things we fuss about ladies, the toilet seat was left up, the toothpaste was left open, you are sleeping in the middle of the bed, you are snatching all the covers in the middle of the night and of course the big one, you are snoring and I can't get any sleep, yes, that's a big one. I let's not leave out the gentlemen, shall we, like, why do you keep moving my stuff when you clean up or maybe it's that you don't clean up. How about the complaints about you nagging all the time, yelling at the kids or you don't cook enough, etc.? Some of these are things that we can fix and adjust with no real effort, but the point is we start voicing all these things to each other that we didn't do when we dated or in the beginning right? What we held our tongue on in the past was now sneaking out of our mouths quicker, and sometimes with a vengeance.

We started to get more comfortable saying what was on my mind but probably a little more relaxed on how it would make him feel or how he would react. I admit, I have my ways, don't we all, but I was making a lot of noise, running my mouth about what I thought wasn't right, and quite frankly ladies, it's not a turn on. I was getting complacent and didn't realize it.

I know that we all have some very legitimate concerns and complaints about the household, kids, finances, etc. but sometimes, maybe even a lot of times, we are talking about it all the time and, what happens when you start talking a lot about the same thing? You stop being heard. I had become a "broken record" and he was getting tired of hearing that same ole' song. It's not that what I was saying wasn't something that needed to be done, it was that I was saying the same thing over and over with no solution.

The big factor in me shutting up was that I had to decide if it was more important that I be right, or did I want to be happy. Of course, we all want to be right, it's human nature, but it wasn't more important than being happy to me. I also found out that the happier we were, the more he gave in and did it my way anyway. How about that. I took the fight and the struggle out of the scenario and it created a new view on things. I wasted a lot of time fighting a battle that I had already won if I had just shut my mouth. Ok! I have shared some ways that shutting your mouth can prove to be a great and positive thing and improve a situation, but I can't talk about the good without talking about the bad right. Let me share a different perspective on how you can abuse the Power of Shut Up.

Well, remember I mentioned that I was the talker in my marriage, well, you may also remember that I mentioned my husband was not, lol. Although we have great conversations, I know some of you ladies can relate to the fact that you do most of the talking, or fussing, as the guys may call it but, none the less it not shutting up. But, using your silence as a weapon is not a good thing. If you are choosing to shut up to punish, dismiss, embarrass, control, or to simply be mean, then you are abusing the Power of Shut Up. And that's not good.

We have all been in arguments with our partners, spouses, etc., but can you recall a time when you were both at odds on an issue and one person wanted to discuss it and the other didn't? You know those time when things got heated, there was no end in sight because everyone was standing their ground. Do you remember the moment when one person finally said something like, "Fine, have it your way" or how about "Whatever" or even, "I don't care" and then all goes quiet, Great right? Maybe not, because while you feel that you have won the fight and are feeling great, the person that gave in is not in a good space at all, but you don't find out until you realize that they aren't speaking to you. You are getting the silent treatment. There has been a shift in the power of shut up. Now what?

My husband was the king of the "silent treatment" and it drove me absolutely batty. I hated the moments when we weren't speaking because of a disagreement and it stressed me to no end. I always thought that ignoring or giving someone the silent treatment was just plain silly. The bad thing was that it worked, on me at least. I hated it. I always felt like if there was something that needed to be addressed that was causing us some strife, let's get it all on the table and figure it out so we could move on. I felt like we were wasting time that could be spent enjoying each other instead of being mad, Great concept, right? Except everybody isn't you. Everybody doesn't think that way you do nor do they do the things you do and frankly, if we understood that more, we would probably find more peace instantly because the expectation would/should change.

Ok, let's get back to this "Silent Treatment" thing! One of my pet peeves, at least it used to be. This is an example of how the Power of Shut up can be used as a weapon against someone. And let's remember, any power can be twisted and used for negative reasons, so you have to make sure you are being responsible once you have it. Many times, I would be in talk mode and he was not, and yes, I would push the conversation which pushed him to rebel, and there you have it, SILENCE. Have you ever been in the middle of a conversation or argument and then suddenly someone decides that they are done talking and go silent? Not because they were finished their sentence but because they were done hearing you speak. He was "taking control" in his way. It could have been several reasons why he stopped talking, some will relate"

➢ They don't want to discuss the subject anymore

- ➤ They are irritated with the energy that the argument is bringing to the conversation
- ➤ They no longer know how to address the situation
- ➤ The conversation/argument is not bringing resolution to the issue

Those are just a few, and you might agree that some of them are good reasons, but, it's all in how you do it that makes using silence as a power, as a punishment. When you silence someone because you decided that you don't want to continue the conversation, please think about how you do accomplish that goal. If you are stopping out of selfishness or to punish someone for forcing a conversation, then take a step back to think about it:

- ❖ How would you feel if someone cut you off the same way?
- ❖ Would you feel disrespected?
- ❖ How would you respond if someone went silent while you were arguing?

Sometimes thinking about how it would make you feel personally can change the way to receive or respond to a situation. In my opinion, Empathy is necessary in so many life lessons, and gaining some Shut Up power is no exception.

REFLECTIONS

Have you ever spoke up about something only to find out that you misunderstood what was being said and you had to take back those words? Share

_____

_____

_____

_____

_____

_____

_____

_____

_____

Let's be very honest – Did you go back and apologize? Did you actually take ownership for speaking to quickly?

Reminder: Thinking before you speak may save you a few apologies 😊

_____

_____

_____

_____

_____

_____

_____

The Power of Shut Up in our Relationships with our Kids

Do we really get through to them when we yell?

We all have those moments where we are completely frustrated because we have been telling someone something over and repeatedly with no resolve or change. We feel like we are giving great advice or that our concern or complaints are legitimate and we push to make others understand our plight. As a matter of fact, we will talk so much sometimes that we even get tired of hearing ourselves speak. I have experienced those times often while going through a difficult situation with my kids, my husband, a friend going through something etc. But, there comes a time when you have to decide to stop.

Well, I can share that I had one of those moments when I was going through some stuff trying to manage a blended family that just wasn't blending. I couldn't get the children to listen, nor my husband and I was at my wits end. I was tired of being the only one to say something about the things that I felt needed to be corrected and I just wanted someone to listen to me. I would yell, holler, and sometimes flip the script and not talk to anyone out of frustration, but the reality was that either way I tried, it produced that same behavior, NOTHING! No one was listening and furthermore, no one cared to listen. I was sounding like a worrisome old step mother who just loved to fuss and complain, and my husband was a little annoyed too. But in my eyes, they had no right to be. I was right and I knew it. Why was no one hearing me? Why were they making me out to be the bad guy? Why was I the only one who cared about getting things done the right way?

I went to a friend to discuss my issues and of course, like we always do, expected her to be on my side. Yes, you know we say we want the truth so, "tell us like it is" but the truth is, we want to hear what we want to hear and we want you to understand and agree with everything we are saying, right? I mean for real, who wants to go to someone to vent and share, only to have them tell you that everything you are saying is wrong and better yet, tell you to "Shut Your Mouth"! Well, it happened to me. Not only did it piss me off, but it brought me to tears. Yes, I cried, right there on the phone in the middle of my conversation. "Excuse me, what do you mean shut my mouth?" How dare she tell me that I should be quiet about somethings that I felt were dead wrong going on and not have anything to say about it! Not only was I mad and insulted, I was totally caught off guard. Like I said, I was looking for another #TeamLisa player. I was venting with the understanding that who I chose to vent to was going to be on my side. I was totally right and totally wrong at the same time.

But, I will explain to you why this was one of the most pivotal points in my understanding of the Power of my voice.

Conclusion

The feeling on the other side is AMAZING! Now, I will be the 1st to tell you that I am always a work in progress and my "Power" is tested sometimes daily, but, I have learned so many things about taking my time to speak, thinking 1st and deciding what I am trying to accomplish when I speak. Too often we can do what is right but instead, we speak! The peace in knowing when to say something and when not to is one of the best gifts that I have developed in my 50 years of life and I am so excited to share it with everyone. I found a great sense of peace and learning how to use my Power of Shut Up!

Life changed for me the moment I realized that a lot of what I went through, experienced, etc. was all about ME! I was bringing a lot of the drama I experienced on myself. My communication skills and understanding skills have gone off the charts ever since I started to master my Power of Shut up! I see things differently, I experience life differently and I will tell you this, the anxiety that I used to have in approaching conversation that most of the time, didn't need to happen, or

111

to stop a conversation long before it gets to a place of chaos or confusion or hurt and pain has definitely changed me for the better. I learned by trial and error, of course but hopefully this book will help you to skip some of the unnecessary steps I made and find peace sooner!

I started to understand that I was exhausting a lot of energy trying to prove what I was or who I was to people who were going to believe what they wanted to believe or do what they wanted to do regardless of what I said. I learned that sometimes all I need to know if that I know if that makes sense. Sometimes those who feel the need to constantly speak up and say something all the time are the same people who are truly not confident in what they are saying. I had to understand that Confidence Speaks without spoken word. Learning to be quiet and Shut Up is possibly the hardest lesson I have ever learned in life, but it has also been the most rewarding.

I realized that most people don't listen to hear what you are saying, they merely wait for their turn to speak. Have you ever noticed when you go into a meeting, and it seems like time was lost because when you leave the meeting, you are not sure what it was about and you also aren't sure what you are supposed to be doing next? You walk away feeling like you don't know any more than you knew when you went in to the meeting. We all have had those moments, but what I think happens sometimes is that we are all so busy talking, trying to make sure our opinions are heard and our thoughts are understood that we don't realize that we all might be on the same page.

Yes, our voices are important, but better than that, they are necessary! But, it's how you use it that makes it powerful.

Communication is the key to all relationships that you encounter from the day you are born until the day you utter your last words. What I want to help everyone to do is to give your best at making sure that every time you use your voice, it brings wisdom, peace and comfort to you and those around you. Words can do so much damage to people and truly guide people in all aspects of their lives. The words that are spoken to you as child will manifest in great ways and bad ways in your life so they are absolutely vital to the way you show up in the world. This book was written to help you guide your way through this journey. The way I viewed myself and the people around me was a direct connect to what my parents said to me when responding or not responding to things I did wrong as well as things I did right. What you say to yourself matters!

I learned to use positive affirmations daily if possible, to get through some of my toughest times in life. I also learned that positive affirmations work as constant reminders to my soul and my psychic that I am enough even when no one else believes it or says it. This journey has been a true eye opener for me and it has blessed my life in an amazing way. Although I am not perfect by any stretch, I have gained some great awareness in what my triggers are and how to counteract those triggers by taking, sometimes as little as one minute, to step away from the situation and assess how I respond. #oneminutematters

Please remember, The Power of Shut up is not about not having a voice, it's about taking control of your voice and how you show up in the world through your actions and words. Communication is the key to just about everything that you will do and encounter in life and learning how to discern when, how and if can prove to be very beneficial in gaining true peace within. We all want to live a life of peace and happiness so anything that will bring that to you is worth a try. I am not suggesting that everything I have mentioned will work for you, nor am I suggested that it will work every single time, but what I am suggesting is that giving these things a try might actually make you feel better about life by removing as much stress as you can in your life.

Positive Affirmations

Sometimes it is what you say to yourself that makes all the difference in how you respond to others. Positive affirmations help you to organize your thought in a way that uplift you and pour into your soul in a motivating way.

- I am strong and fearless, and I will no longer let things that do not move me forward control my words, thoughts or deeds

- I will not always get it right, but that is ok because it is never too late to start over again.

- I will stay focused on my goals and stop giving attention to distractions that take me in the opposite direction.

Shut Up Quotes

We spend the first twelve months of our children's lives teaching them to walk and talk and the next twelve telling them to sit down and shut up.

Phyllis Diller

Much talking is the cause of danger. Silence is the means of avoiding misfortune. The talkative parrot is shut up in a cage. Other birds, without speech, fly freely about.

Sakya Pandita

Always do sober what you said you'd do drunk. That will teach you to keep your mouth shut.

Ernest Hemingway

"It is better to keep your mouth shut and appear stupid, than to open it and remove all doubt."

Mark Twain

Here is some simple advice found in the Bible as to when to keep your mouth shut!

- In the heat of anger. ~ Proverbs 14:17.
- When you don't have all the facts .~ Proverbs 18:13.
- When you haven't verified the story. ~Deuteronomy 17:6.
- If your words will offend a weaker brother. ~ 1 Corinthians 8:11.
- When you are tempted to joke about sin. ~ Proverbs 14:9.
- When you would be ashamed of your words later. ~ Proverbs 8:8.
- When you're tempted to make light of holy things. ~ Ecclesiastes 5:2.
- If your words would convey a wrong impression. ~ Proverbs 17:27.
- If the issue is none of your business. ~ Proverbs 14:10.
- When you are tempted to tell an outright lie. ~Proverbs 4:24.
- If your words will damage someone's reputation. ~Proverbs 16:27.
- If your words will destroy a friendship. ~Proverbs 25:28.
- When you are feeling critical. ~ James 3:9.
- When it is time to listen. ~ Proverbs 13:1.
- If you may have to eat your words later. ~Proverbs 18:21.
- If you have already said it more than one time and then it becomes nagging. ~Proverbs 19:13.
- When you are tempted to flatter a wicked person. ~ Proverbs 24:24.
- When you are supposed to be working instead. ~ Proverbs 14:23

Acknowledgements

To my husband,

Thank you from the bottom of my heart for your strength and love! It takes a special patience and love to handle a creative mind and I want to say "Thank You" for sharing this journey with me. We have been through so much and no matter what, we have done it together. You have been my sounding board, my shoulder and my right hand through everything and I appreciate the way you hold me down no matter what. I am blessed and grateful that God chose you for me and that he chose this journey for us. You are my ROCK and I LOVE YOU! Hold on tight because this is just the beginning, baby. We got this! #TeamWashington

To my Beautiful SHERO,

There will never be enough words to express how thankful and blessed I am to be able to call you Mommy! You are the reason that I will always know that "This too shall pass"! You have inspired me in more ways than you know to make my dreams a reality! Thank you for always believing in me and instilling in me a everything I need to believe in myself! You love is like no other and I love you endlessly. No matter what, you are always there. Thank you for being a firm, faithful, determined, and strong woman. I learned from the BEST! One of the reasons I believed I could do anything I set my mind to and did it was because you did. To my biggest fan, thank you for always lifting me higher! You made me believe in Me!

I Love you Mommy!

After tapping into her gifts and going after her dreams, Lisa Dove Washington has become a Media Entrepreneur whose services are in demand for her highly-recognized skills in social media marketing, event coverage, interviewing, and much more.

Since the age of 12, Lisa has used her gift of gab to accomplish many things, including becoming the advice columnist for Dear Asil (Lisa spelled backwards). After graduating from high school, she attended Spelman College in Atlanta to major in English with a minor in Communications.

Lisa is the publisher of her global online magazine, *Dove Style Magazine*, which she launched in 2012 following her job as a contributing writer for *Celebrity Charity Magazine* out of California. She is sought after for her public relations skills and has had the opportunity to interview a variety of celebrities, such as Stacy Lattisaw Jackson, Donald Lawrence, Tanya Blount, and Reverend Joseph Lowery to name a few, as well as doing features on local talent, foundations, and businesses from all over the country.

Lisa's list of accomplishments includes co-authoring two publications, *The Global Red Circle: Standing in Truth, Unleashing Our Most Powerful Selves* by Kim Andrews and *Artificial Beaute: The True Beaute Beneath the Surface – A Woman's Anthology* by Bonita Parker. Also, she edited a book from the extensive For Dummies series titled *Bowling for Dummies* written by A.J. Forrest and Lisa Iannucci. Touching on her acting abilities, Lisa was cast in several web series and the movie *C.E.O. (Criminal Enterprise Organization)* produced by Antwon Temoney.

Sought after to promote events via social media and provide event promotions and publicity, Lisa is putting her God-given gifts to work, and she is just getting started. Currently, Lisa is the co-host of the Girls Gabbin' Radio Show that airs every Sunday at 7:00 pm (EST) on WINDC Radio powered by GoWin Media. Her goal is to empower, enlighten, and inspire others to shine while living their dreams.

Lisa serves as a committee member of the Ebenezer Institute at Ebenezer A.M.E. United Methodist Church in Fort Washington, Maryland. The Ebenezer Institute was created to give the community options to enhance their education and skills. Lisa also serves on the Advisory Board for the STEM program at her former high school, H.D. Woodson High School, and is an active member and mentor of the "I Love Me" mentoring program founded by Ms. Darcel Collins in Maryland. The "I Love Me" program assists young women with educational, social, emotional, and professional enlightenment with an emphasis on the power of the mind, and Lisa feels blessed to be a part of the organization.

A native of Washington DC, Lisa is a devoted wife and the proud mother of two.

Contact Info:
Website: www.lisadovewashington.com
Email: Mrsldwashington@gmail.com
Facebook - Lisa Dove Washington
Instagram -@lisadovewashington
Twitter- @LWashingtonCCM

CPSIA information can be obtained
at www.ICGtesting.com
Printed in the USA
BVHW021915220419
546200BV00018B/275/P

9 780960 048328